play like

Audio Access Included!

Robert Johnson

The Ultimate Guitar Lesson

by Dave Rubin

Robert Johnson Studio Portrait
Hooks Bros., Memphis, circa 1935
© 1989 Delta Haze Corporation
All Rights Reserved. Used By Permission.

PLAYBACK+
Speed • Pitch • Balance • Loop

To access audio visit:
www.halleonard.com/mylibrary

"Enter Code"
6836-6436-3188-1718

ISBN: 978-1-4950-7666-4

Visit Hal Leonard Online at
www.halleonard.com

Contact Us:
Hal Leonard
7777 West Bluemound Road
Milwaukee, WI 53213
Email: info@halleonard.com

In Europe contact:
Hal Leonard Europe Limited
42 Wigmore Street
Marylebone, London, W1U 2RN
Email: info@halleonardeurope.com

In Australia contact:
Hal Leonard Australia Pty. Ltd.
4 Lentara Court
Cheltenham, Victoria, 3192 Australia
Email: info@halleonard.com.au

CONTENTS

INTRODUCTION

His legend would not grow until after the myth of him selling his soul to the devil at the "crossroads" in exchange for musical dominance gained traction in the 1960s, long after his death. However, Robert Johnson, through his music, had the ability to move souls, beginning in the 1930s. It continues on down to the current day due to his superior combination of advanced technical skills and original blues songs, which indeed seem supernatural in their hypnotic power.

When Keith Richards first heard Robert Johnson, he mistakenly thought there were two guitarists playing. Now, the ability to tap into the seeming sleight-of-hand of this "one-man blues band" is before you. The following chapters will guide you, step by step, down the Delta blues highway to the real blues guitar "Crossroads." So, pick up your axe, acoustic or electric, and let the "Walkin'" and "Ramblin'" blues commence.

Gear: The Holy Grails of Acoustic Blues Guitar

The three available photos of Robert Johnson show him with three different flat-top acoustic guitars, two of which assisted his "Preachin' (the) Blues."

Songs

Five complete monumental Delta blues display the unsurpassed skill and shamanistic power of the "Phantom."

Essential Licks

Despite having a "Hell Hound on [His] Trail," Johnson found time to develop a compendium of the tastiest licks that every blues and blues-rock guitarist should know, and here resides the best to be learned and lived.

Signature Riffs

The immortal riffs of "Robert Dusty," which closed out the Delta blues era and forecasted postwar acoustic and electric blues.

Integral Techniques

Go deep and wide into what makes his songs so vital to guitarists after 80 years.

Stylistic DNA

Hidden secrets behind the "Steady Rollin' Man" revealed.

Must Hear

There are only 29 known Robert Johnson recordings in existence. There have been many different releases of them since the early '60s. Here are the best—and why.

Must See

"The story that never ends" seemed to have an astounding chapter in the late '90s, when a startling film of Johnson playing on a Mississippi street began making the rounds, a clip that this author saw in person early on. Alas, though bearing a remarkable and tantalizing resemblance, it is clearly not him, as he died in 1938 and the documentary, from which it was nefariously snipped, was shot in 1941. Hence, blues fans are left with only photos to glimpse his image frozen in time.

ABOUT THE AUDIO

To access the audio examples that accompany this book, simply go to **www.halleonard.com/mylibrary** and enter the code found on page 1. This will give you instant access to every example. The examples that include audio are marked with an audio icon throughout the book.

GEAR:
THE HOLY GRAILS OF ACOUSTIC BLUES GUITAR

Gibson L-1 (circa 1929)

Featured in the Hicks Bros. studio portrait in which Johnson is nattily attired in a pinstriped suit and fedora, the L-1 was introduced in 1926 as a budget flat-top. It began like the less-expensive L-0, as a small "parlor" guitar with a narrow waist, and measured 13-1/2" at the widest point on the lower bout. By 1929, it had grown to 14-3/4" wide like the L-2, while still retaining the 12-fret neck. In 1932, it was stretched to 14 frets clear of the body, and manufactured until 1937.

The L-1 offered quality construction, balanced tone, and playability with the "short" Gibson scale of 24-3/4", along with affordability to guitarists in the Depression-era South. Thin woods, braces, and lacquer finishes contributed to the wonderful responsiveness and resonance of these little gems. The price to be paid for this featherweight construction, however, is the fragility and tendency to self-destruct if strung with gauges heavier than acoustic light (.012s).

Judging from the sound and lack of a capo on Johnson's last two sessions in Dallas, 1937, it appears he used the L-1 on "I'm a Steady Rollin' Man," "Hell Hound on My Trail," "Stop Breakin' Down Blues," and "Love in Vain Blues."

Gibson L-00 (circa 1935–36)

The "Photo Booth" self-portrait shows a cropped guitar, which seems problematic in making positive identification. It would have been helpful, of course, if the headstock was visible, along with more of the body. In lieu of that, however, the available evidence points to the L-00.

Introduced around 1930, the L-00 was a 14-fret model with the same body dimensions as the other L-series guitars, including the L-1. Initially finished entirely in black lacquer, it acquired a small sunburst in 1934 and back binding in 1937. In addition, these later models all had a position marker at fret 15. The "Photo Booth" picture shows a guitar without back binding or a marker at fret 15, thereby matching the 1935–36 L-00 exactly. Coincidentally, it also looks like the 14-fret Kalamazoo guitars of the era made by Gibson. However, they were not manufactured until 1938, the year of Johnson's death.

It is believed that Johnson used the 14-fret L-00 during four sessions in San Antonio in 1936, on "Kind Hearted Woman," "I Believe I'll Dust My Broom," "Sweet Home Chicago," "Ramblin' on My Mind," "Come on in My Kitchen," "Terraplane Blues," "32–20 Blues," "Cross Road Blues," "Walkin' Blues," "Preachin' Blues," and "If I Had Possession over Judgment Day."

Addenda

The late Mac McCormick had in his possession another photo of Johnson taken in the Hicks Bros. studio, seen briefly from a distance by Peter Guralnick. It is assumed that it also shows his L-1. In addition, a photo believed to be Johnson and Johnny Shines posing in a studio was bought on eBay in 2008. It shows Johnson with what appears to be a "prop" flat-top from the era, sans strings.

Thumb Pick

As detailed in the "Integral Techniques" section, Johnson was known to have played fingerstyle, using a thumb pick and bare fingers.

SONGS

Kind Hearted Woman Blues
Recorded Monday, November 23, 1936, in San Antonio, Texas

As a true blues guitar hero who strutted his stuff with swagger, Johnson began his first recording session with his first masterpiece. "Kind Hearted Woman Blues" is performed with ease, perhaps confirming it as one of his oldest and most-played compositions. Besides being his only recorded song with an instrumental break or solo, amazingly it is also one of only two songs to become a "hit" in his lifetime. It is partly due to his short time as a recording artist coming at the end of the Delta blues era, as well as to electric guitars looming on the horizon. Though impossible to prove, and from a somewhat dubious source, Memphis blues musician Earl Bell claimed to the late Steve LaVere to have seen Robert play electric guitar with a bassist and a drummer who had "Robert Johnson" painted on his bass drum head.

Intro

The song's three-measure intro also serves as an introduction to one of his most basic techniques: accentuating select notes from standard blues chord forms. Be aware that it is often referred to as his "double turnaround," and that measure 1, played in 6/4 time, would be seen and played by modern blues guitarists as two measures of 4/4 time. Below is a selection of the implied chords expanded to full voicings.

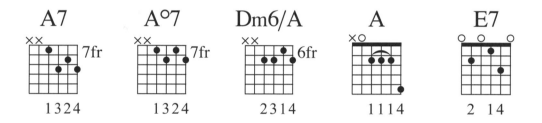

Performance Tip: "Robert Johnson 101" is his use of an index—or even middle—finger barre on the bass strings. The former is clearly employed for the A major chord and could be used for the A7.

Measures 2–3 contain the classic Robert Johnson descending turnaround pattern. Here is a streamlined version, as it is commonly played today:

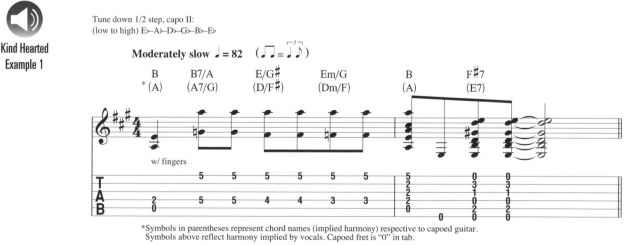

Kind Hearted Example 1

*Symbols in parentheses represent chord names (implied harmony) respective to capoed guitar.
Symbols above reflect harmony implied by vocals. Capoed fret is "0" in tab.

Performance Tip: In measure 1, anchor the pinky on string 1 (A) and walk down on string 4 with the ring (G), middle (F#), and index (F) fingers. In measure 2, resolve to the A major voicing with the index as a barre and the pinky remaining on string 1 in what was not a stretch for Johnson with those long, spidery fingers seen in the "Photo Booth" picture!

Verse 1

Within a stunning example of Delta blues chock full of signature licks, the verse features harmonic forms in measures 4–7 of the I chord (A7) seemingly without precedent. It involves implied movement from A7 to A°7 via a delicate, "chimey" effect appropriate for honoring a "kind hearted" woman who nonetheless does not love him and "does evil all the time"! Though Johnson is only picking the most crucial melody notes in measure 4, such as the 3rd (C♯) and ♭5th (E♭), the implication is one of A7 to A°7 and back to A7 (see below). The change of A°7 back to A7 from beat 4 of measure 6 to beat 1 of measure 7 is dramatic, making the forward momentum to the IV chord (D7/F♯) in measure 8 that much more pronounced.

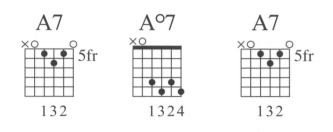

The dynamic usage of single notes and dyads on the top strings, combined with open bass strings and cut boogie patterns, is a hallmark of Johnson's "mojo."

The IV chord in measures 8–9 and 13 is a staple of prewar and postwar blues and another instance of the way Johnson often selects only the most important notes of a chord voicing to impart the desired musical information.

Johnson likely used this fingering for the IV chord:

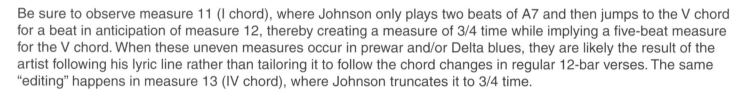

Be sure to observe measure 11 (I chord), where Johnson only plays two beats of A7 and then jumps to the V chord for a beat in anticipation of measure 12, thereby creating a measure of 3/4 time while implying a five-beat measure for the V chord. When these uneven measures occur in prewar and/or Delta blues, they are likely the result of the artist following his lyric line rather than tailoring it to follow the chord changes in regular 12-bar verses. The same "editing" happens in measure 13 (IV chord), where Johnson truncates it to 3/4 time.

Performance Tip: The majority of contemporary guitarists will arrange the verses to contain 12 measures in standard 4/4 time.

Measure 14, the turnaround, exhibits a subtle yet important nuance derived from his fingering technique, whereby Johnson takes advantage of those exceptionally long digits: though he is mainly plucking strings 4 and 1, by the time he gets to beats 3 and 4, it is clear something else is going on, as the A note on string 3 appears. In order to logically access it while maintaining hand position for the notes on strings 4 and 1, it would seem necessary to barre fret 2 with the index finger from string 1 to string 4.

Performance Tip: Scale length will have an effect on making the necessary stretch, especially when beginning at fret 5 on string 4 with the ring finger, while the pinky holds down the root on string 1 at fret 5. For example, the standard Gibson length on electrics and acoustics is shorter than that of Martin guitars, as well as Fender Strats and Teles. In addition, since the use of the index for the F note at fret 3 will be lost with the index anchored at fret 2, it is recommended to utilize the ring finger for both the G and the F♯ notes and the middle finger for the F note (see photos).

Bridge

Johnson smartly inserts dramatic stop-time in measures 27–30 of the bridge, which follows verse 2 and precedes the guitar solo. Besides providing rhythmic contrast to his steady shuffling verses, stop-time allows him to lyrically highlight his excuse for drinking, which he blames on the woman. Gaining more mileage from the A7 and A°7 forms, he efficiently edits them down to fretted notes on strings 4 and 3 and the open fifth string. Hence, all he needs to do to transition from A7 to A°7 is to move C♯/G at frets 5–6 to C/G♭ at frets 4–5.

Though it may be open to conjecture, it appears measures 31–32, which would normally contain the IV chord, are actually two more measures of the I chord. The notes seem to bear this out if they are expanded harmonically to the chord forms below and played in both measures.

**Kind Hearted
Example 2**

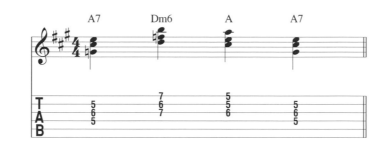

In a way, measures 31–32 individually resemble the descending turnaround in measure 37, though the former implies harmony relative to the I chord rather than a I–IV–I progression. Observe the way Johnson edits his forms down to the bare minimum with single notes in measure 32 while still implying the same harmony.

Be sure to check out measure 36 (IV chord), where Johnson slips in a second inversion (5th on bottom) D7/A chord. For reference purposes, the chord frames below show root position, first inversion, second inversion, and third inversion (♭7th on bottom) D7 voicings common to the blues.

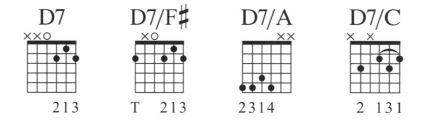

Guitar Solo

As previously stated, Johnson only recorded one solo, or instrumental break. An uneven 11 measures long, in part due to measure 46 being in 6/4 time, it nonetheless is a Delta blues guitar landmark of composition and expressive phrasing. He continues to blend treble-string licks and accompaniment chord forms like a magician with impeccable prestidigitation skills, as well as conjure choice note combinations that flow from the harmony.

Upon closer study, it will be apparent that the guitar solo is a variation of the verses in form and structure. However, Johnson subtly manipulates the elements by adding fills in just the right amount, and in just the right places, to produce the stunning effect of two guitars weaving a rich sonic tapestry.

In measures 39–40 (I chord), he walks down from A7 to A with a combination of A7 triple stops, an implied Dm6 chord (measure 40, beat 2), and thumping bass strings holding the bottom together. In measure 41, he drives the momentum forward with pumping A7 triple stops strummed in triplets. He follows in measure 42 with yet another creative variation on the descending pattern in measure 40, which serves to function as a way to connect smoothly to the IV chord in measures 43–44. Once locked in at fret 2, Johnson literally creates two measures of chord melody. He picks descending lines of C (♭7th) and A (5th), which repeat in measure 44, with the addition of resolution to the open fourth string (D = root), all the while maintaining steady quarter notes via partial first-inversion D7 voicings on the bottom strings.

Measures 45–49 are essentially the same as those in the verse. However, Johnson picks more notes within the changes to fill up and enhance the space where the vocals would normally reside.

KIND HEARTED WOMAN BLUES

Words and Music by Robert Johnson

Kind Hearted
Full Song

* Tune down 1/2 step, capo II:
(low to high) E♭–A♭–D♭–G♭–B♭–E♭

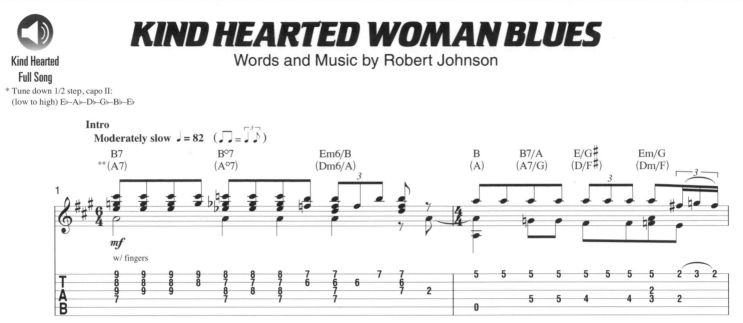

**Symbols in parentheses represent chord names (implied harmony) respective to capoed guitar.
Symbols above reflect harmony implied by vocals. Capoed fret is "0" in tab.

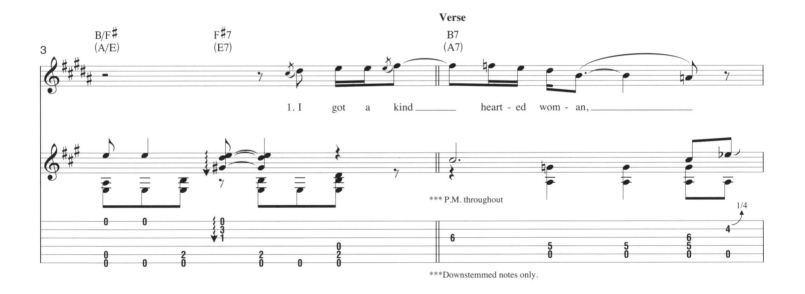

***Downstemmed notes only.

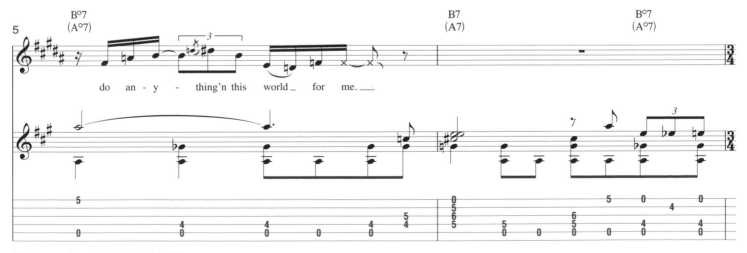

*Tunings were determined using the original 78s.

*Discontinue palm muting downstemmed notes.

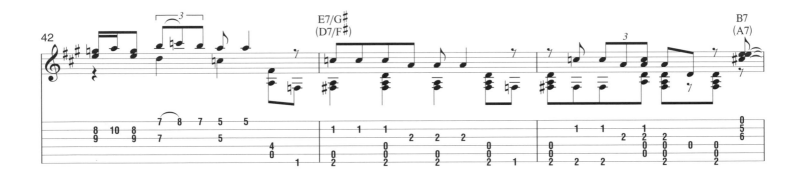

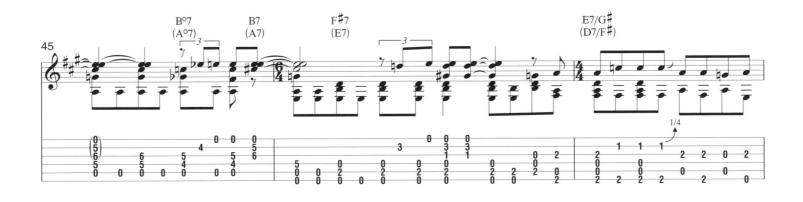

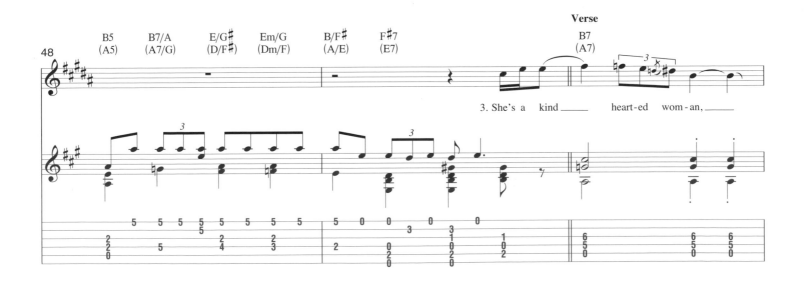

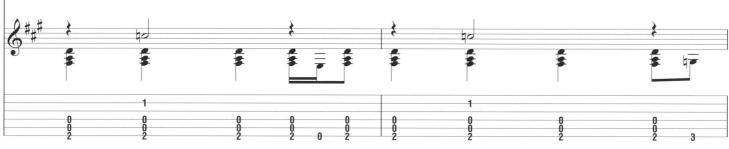

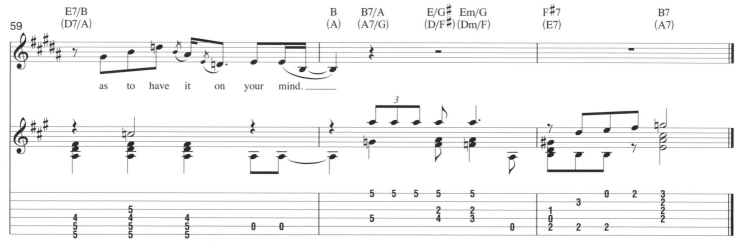

I Believe I'll Dust My Broom
Recorded Monday, November 23, 1936, in San Antonio, Texas

Along with "Sweet Home Chicago," "I Believe I'll Dust My Broom" is one of the most influential blues guitar songs of all time. The signature triplet riff, likely influenced by blues piano and alternating with a cut boogie pattern, became a template for countless blues and rock songs. In 1951, Elmore James built on the Johnson version to create his own landmark electric slide guitar classic.

"Phonograph Blues" (Take 2) contains virtually the same musical forms and is the only other track to contain the Aadd9 tuning. It is a wonder Johnson did not utilize it in more of his compositions, as it allows cut boogie patterns with the root on string 6 (like open E and open D tunings), and chordal forms on strings 3–1 (like open A and open G) for the fullest possible accompaniment. In addition, and this is critical, they may be accessed at the same fret positions.

Intro
Notice the exceedingly cool B9 voicing that appears in measure 2:

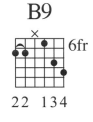

B9

Performance Tip: You may need fingers as long as Johnson's to comfortably access this chord, but try it anyway (see photo). Low to high: barre strings 6 and 5 with the middle finger (see a similar grip in Johnson's "Photo Booth" photo), followed by the index, ring, and pinky fingers.

Verse 1
Measures 3–6 (I chord, E7) immediately shows the brilliance of the Aadd9 tuning, as a credible E7 voicing is easily produced by barring strings 2 and 1 at fret 10 (D/B = $\flat$7th/5th) in conjunction with the open fourth string (E = root).

E7

The cut boogie patterns alternating in measures 4 and 6 (in "call and response" fashion) are a snap with the chordal forms. Measures 7–8 (IV chord, A7) are even more intriguing with the cut boogie pattern on string 6 and 5 and the C$\sharp$ (3rd) and A (root) notes located on strings 1 and 2, respectively.

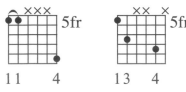

It's another stretch, with the pinky reaching the C♯ and A notes, but more in the mortal realm, especially on a short-scale Gibson or similar guitar.

Dust My Broom
Example 1

Aadd9 tuning, down 1/2 step:
(low to high) E♭–B♭–E♭–A♭–C–E♭

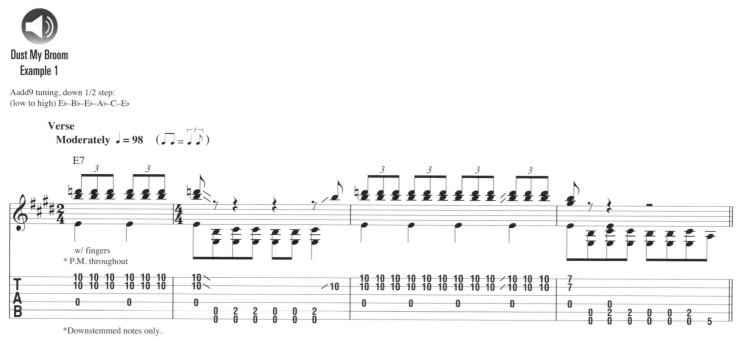

*Downstemmed notes only.

Measure 11 (V chord, B7) demonstrates another great advantage of the unique tuning, as the cut boogie pattern, played efficiently with the index barring strings 6 and 5 at fret 7 for the 5th and the ring finger adding the 6th on string 5, can also present the root on string 1 at fret 7 if the index finger barres completely across all six strings.

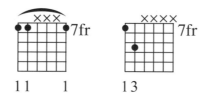

Note how these forms are completely moveable like standard six-string barre chords.

Dust My Broom
Example 2

Aadd9 tuning, down 1/2 step:
(low to high) E♭–B♭–E♭–A♭–C–E♭

Verse 2

Check out measure 21 (I chord) for a masterstroke. Deciding he needed some "blues note" funk, Johnson drops the 5th (B) at fret 10 of string 2 to the ♭5th (B♭) at fret 9 while raising the ♭7th (D) on string 1 up to the root (E). He follows this by resolving to E/B (root/5th) and then back to the signature D/B (♭7th/5th), resulting in one of the most classic and iconic blues guitar riffs of all time. Elmore James would appropriate it and transpose it to slide guitar in open D for his electric guitar version in 1951.

Performance Tip: Play E/A♯ with the pinky and index fingers, moving the index up to fret 10 for E/B before quickly shifting back to D/B with the index barre. However, observe how E/B on beat 4 of measure 7 may be played by just adding the ring finger to fret 12 of string 1.

Dust My Broom
Example 3

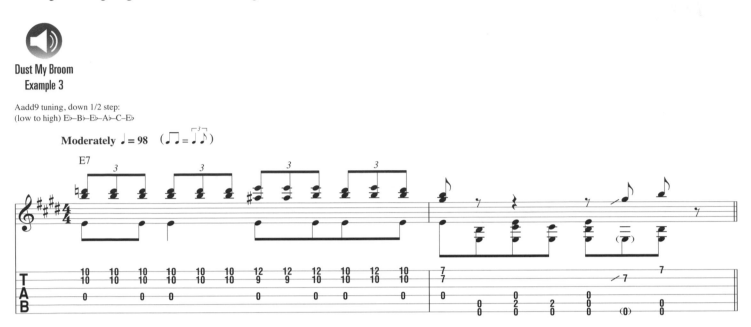

Verse 6
Compare E/B and E7/B in standard tuning to the same chords in Aadd9 tuning (as seen in the very last measure):

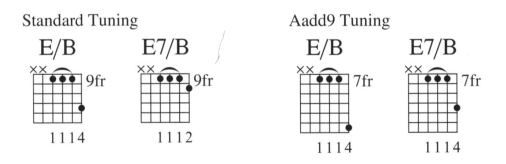

Performance Tip: This is one of the few instances where standard tuning would make for easier fingerings. In Aadd9, barre fret 7 with the index, reaching the E and D notes on string 1 with the pinky.

I BELIEVE I'LL DUST MY BROOM

Words and Music by Robert Johnson

Dust My Broom
Full Song

*Aadd9 tuning, down 1/2 step:
(low to high) E♭–B♭–E♭–A♭–C–E♭

*Tunings were determined using the original 78s.

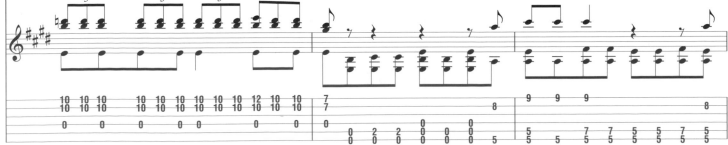

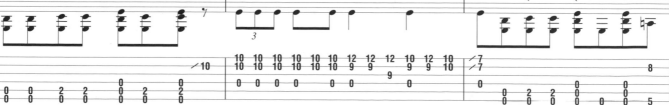

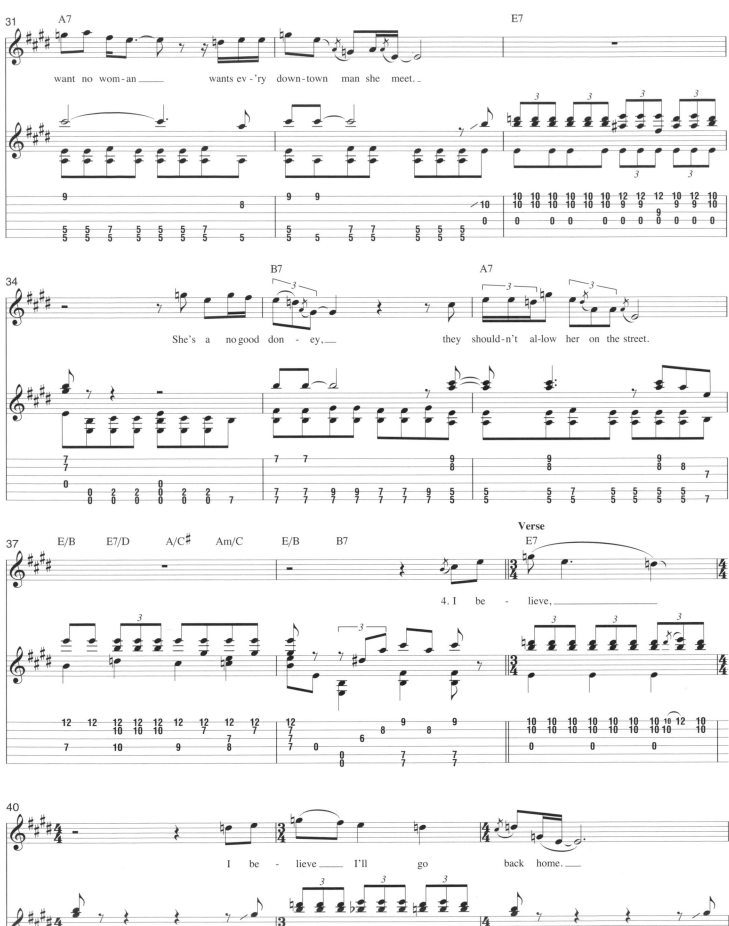

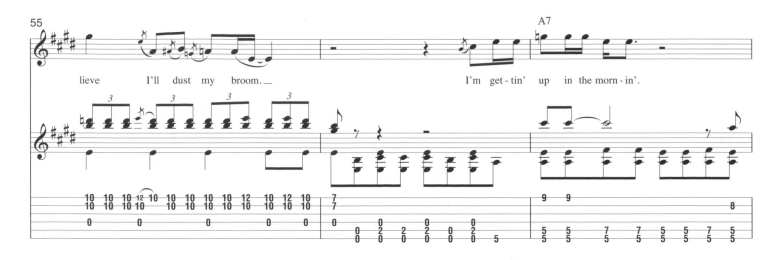

lieve I'll dust my broom. _____ I'm get-tin' up in the morn-in'.

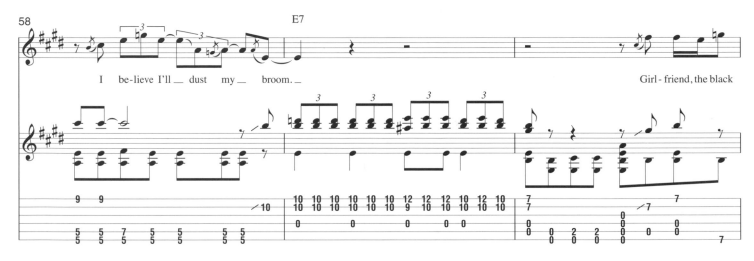

I be-lieve I'll __ dust my __ broom. _____ Girl-friend, the black

man you been lov-in', girl-friend, can get my room.

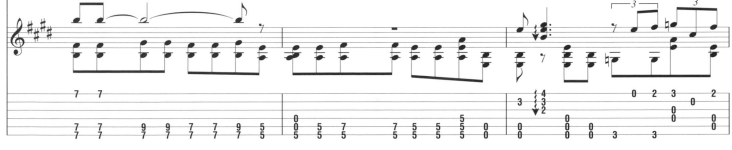

Verse

6. I'm gon' call up Chin-ey, see is my

good girl o - ver there, _____ I'm gon' call up Chin-a, _____ see is

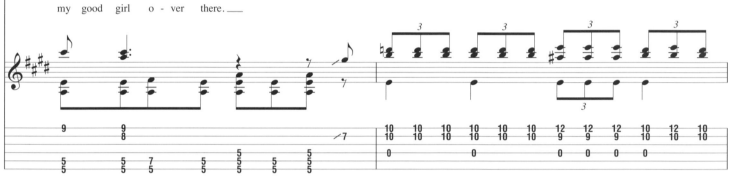

my good girl o - ver there. _____

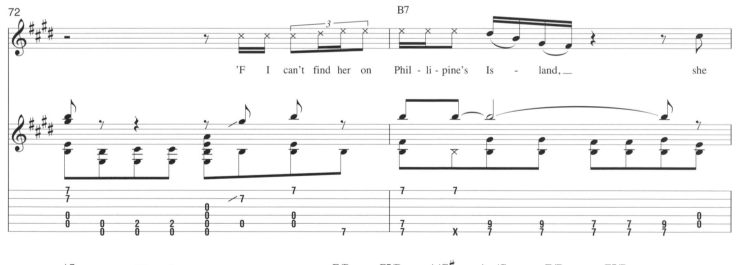

'F I can't find her on Phil - li - pine's Is - land, _____ she

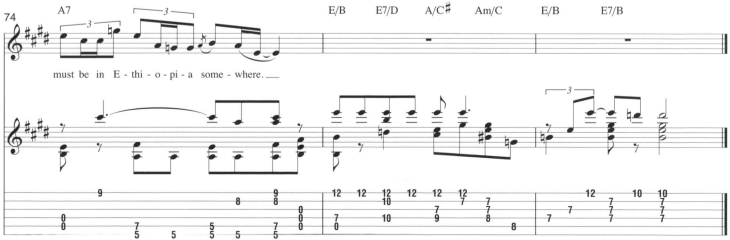

must be in E - thi - o - pi - a some - where. _____

Sweet Home Chicago
Recorded Monday, November 23, 1936, in San Antonio, Texas

Like "Kind Hearted Woman Blues," "Sweet Home Chicago" is in standard tuning. However, it was not a "hit" like "Kind Hearted Woman Blues" or "Terraplane Blues." Nonetheless, it got the attention of his peers and has gone on to undeniable classic status as an evergreen performed and recorded regularly, even today. It is virtually the template for all succeeding boogie blues. And though it may be considered "entry level" Robert Johnson, it contains the essence of boogie blues. Incidentally, "When You Got a Good Friend" employs almost the exact same accompaniment.

Intro

Following his patented descending turnaround pattern in measure 1, in measure 2, Johnson resolves to a second inversion (5th on bottom) B7 voicing to add some lower-register heft.

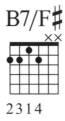

B7/F♯

2 3 1 4

Verses 1 and 2

The first two verses contain the "fast change," moving from the I chord (E7) to the IV chord (A7) in measures 1 and 2. Though Johnson was tuned down a half step and capoed at fret 2, making it sound in the key of F, most blues guitarists today opt to play it in the key of E with open-string cut boogie patterns as shown. His "chugging locomotive" groove, with noticeable accents on each downbeat, is the benchmark for cut boogie patterns and he pretty much lets his accompaniment carry the day. There are few embellishments, or ornaments, but one prominent exception is the transition from measure 5 to measure 6 (I chord), where Johnson inserts a fill with the open first and second strings, which is so perfectly executed as to sound like an overdub.

Sweet Home Chicago Example 1

Tune down 1/2 step, capo II:
(low to high) E♭–A♭–D♭–G♭–B♭–E♭

Moderately ♩ = 94

*Symbols in parentheses represent chord names (implied harmony) respective to capoed guitar.
Symbols above reflect harmony implied by vocals. Capoed fret is "0" in tab.

Performance Tip: If playing with bare fingers or fingerpicks as your preferred technique, perform the boogie bass-string patterns with the thumb or "pinch" the strings with the thumb and index finger. Play the open first and third strings with the middle finger (see photo).

Verses 3–6

When Johnson begins showing off his "math skills" in verses 3, 4, and 5, he alters his 12-bar blues progression to the "slow change," with the first four measures of each containing just the I chord. Though essentially the same accompaniment in each verse, in measure 30 (verse 3), he adds a bit of blues harmony by plucking string 3 (G) open on seven of eight eighth notes. Subtle though it may be, and perhaps subconscious on his part, it nonetheless contributes a small level of richness to that one measure and is worth filing away for one's bag of blues tricks.

Sweet Home
Chicago
Example 2

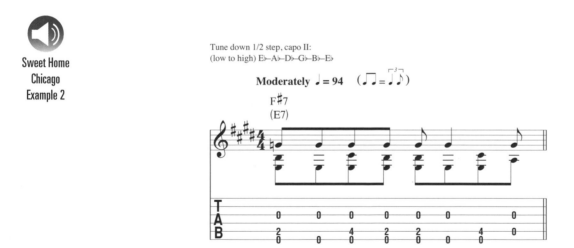

Performance Tip: As with the previous example, access string 3 with the middle finger. Be aware how Johnson also judiciously grabs the open third string in verse 6, along with string 1 chiming open on beat 1 of measures 66–69.

Sweet Home
Chicago
Full Song

SWEET HOME CHICAGO
Words and Music by Robert Johnson

* Tune down 1/2 step, capo II:
(low to high) E♭–A♭–D♭–G♭–B♭–E♭

**Symbols in parentheses represent chord names (implied harmony) respective to capoed guitar.
Symbols above reflect harmony implied by vocals. Capoed fret is "0" in tab.

***Downstemmed notes only.

*Tunings were determined using the original 78s.

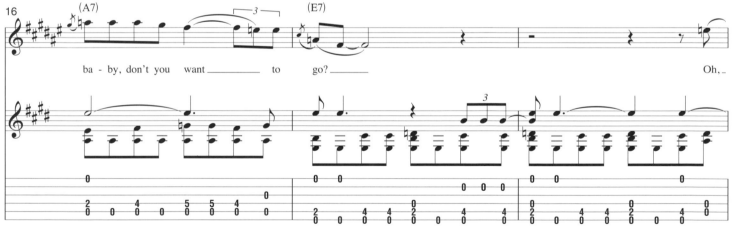

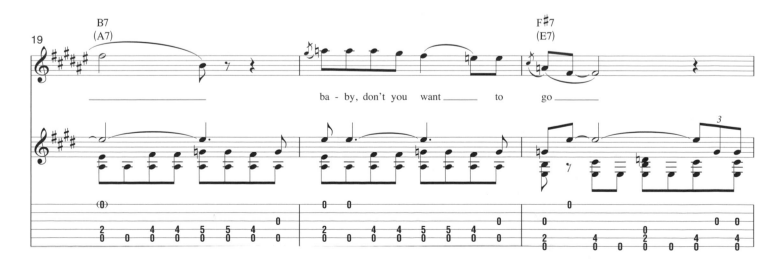

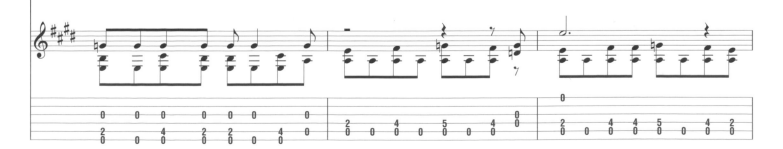

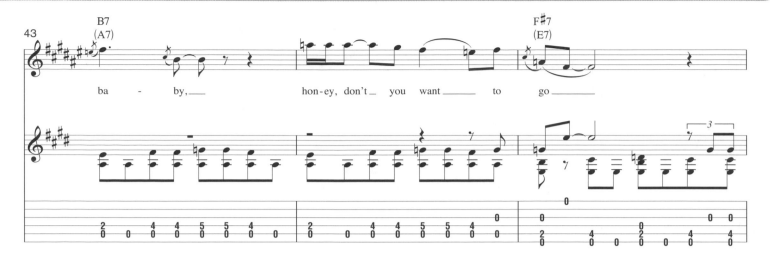

ba - by,___ hon-ey, don't__ you want_____ to go_____

back to the land of Cal - i - for - nia,___ to my sweet home,_ Chi - ca - go?_

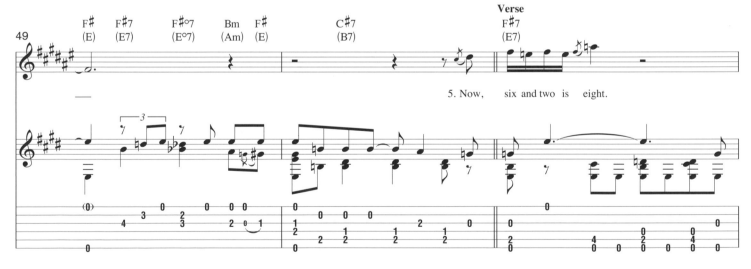

Verse

5. Now, six and two is eight.

Eight and two is ten.   Friend - boy, she trick you one time, she

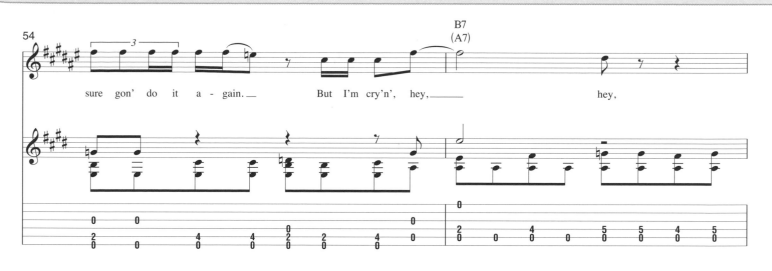

sure gon' do it a - gain.___ But I'm cry'n', hey,___ hey,

ba - by, don't you want___ to go___ to the land

of Cal - i - for - nia,___ to my sweet home,___ Chi - ca - go?___

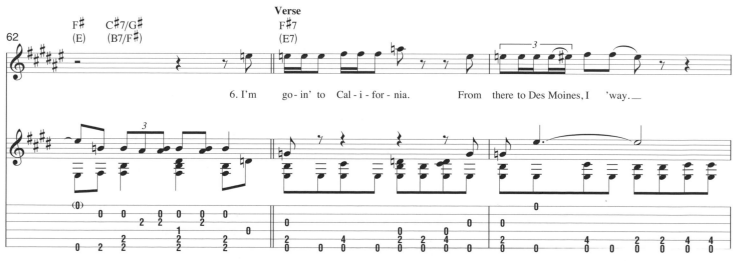

Verse

6. I'm go - in' to Cal - i - for - nia. From there to Des Moines, I 'way.___

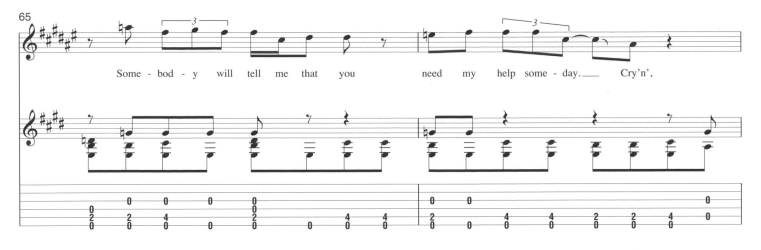

Some - bod - y will tell me that you need my help some - day.___ Cry'n',

hey, hey,___ ba - by, don't you want ___ to go ___

back to the land of Cal - i - for - nia, to my sweet home,_____ Chi - ca - go? _

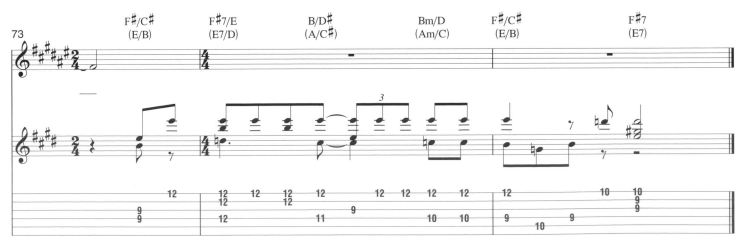

Come on in My Kitchen
Recorded Monday, November 23, 1936, in San Antonio, Texas

Myth or fact, there exists a famous Robert Johnson story as told by Johnny Shines: "His guitar seemed to talk—repeat and say words with him like no one else in the world could. This sound affected most women in a way I could never understand. One time in St. Louis, we were playing one of the songs that Robert would like to play with someone once in a while, 'Come on in My Kitchen.' He was playing very slow and passionately, and when we quit, I noticed no one was saying anything. Then I realized they were crying—both men and women."

Never more romantic pleading ever appeared in a blues and with such conviction. And, as Shines related, the guitar expresses it as much as the heartfelt vocal. A true, timeless landmark of Delta blues slide guitar.

Intro

Open A was Johnson's default open tuning and he proves his mastery of it in a composition which, except for one measure of the V chord (E7) in verse 4, seems to be based only on the I chord (A7). The intro contains a pickup and a measure of A chord forms to establish the tonality, followed by a two-measure descending turnaround pattern—albeit voiced on the lower strings much differently than most of his others—with resolution to the I chord instead of the V.

Notice the use of octaves between the E strings (6 and 4) on beats 2, 3, and 4 of measure 2 to add depth and bottom.

Come on in
My Kitchen
Example 1

Open A tuning, down 1/2 step, capo II:
(low to high) E♭–A♭–E♭–A♭–C–E♭

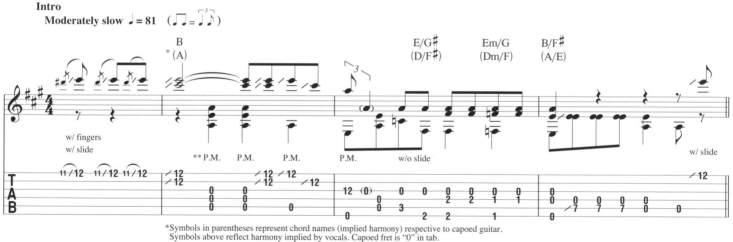

*Symbols in parentheses represent chord names (implied harmony) respective to capoed guitar.
Symbols above reflect harmony implied by vocals. Capoed fret is "0" in tab.

**Downstemmed notes only.

It can be helpful to know open A as based around an A major triad on strings 3–1 in the open position and at the octave:

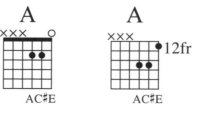

In addition, open A is the same relative tuning as open G, except it involves tuning strings 4, 3, and 2 up a whole step from standard, whereas G requires tuning strings 6, 5, and 1 down a whole step. This should not be taken lightly when dealing with older guitars, especially vintage acoustics with thin tops and old bridges.

Performance Tip: It is always recommended to wear the slider on the pinky finger in order to free up the other three fingers for fretting purposes (see photo). It is literally a necessity in this song, as seen right off in measures 2 and 3.

Verse 1

Note that verses 1, 2, and 4 are 10 measures long, while verse 3 contains eight measures and verse 5 has nine. The bridge, which is essentially the same monochord progression as the verses, has 11 measures. One distinct advantage of having the entire song predicated on the I chord is how easy it is to expand or contract the length of the verses via adding or subtracting lyrics.

Part of Johnson's musical genius, and it is not hyperbole, is shown by the way he seemingly implies other harmonies throughout while still operating within the bounds of the A major tonality. Check out how this is reinforced by his choice of vocal notes (in the key of B♭ as heard on the recording and shown in the transcription): in measures 4–5, he is clearly on the I chord (B♭) while he emphasizes the root (B♭) and major 3rd (D) notes. In measures 6–7, however, he seems to imply the IV chord (E♭) with the root (E♭), 4th (A♭), 5th (B♭), and ♭7th (D♭). In measure 8, he is back on the I chord with the 3rd (D) and root (B♭). Measures 9–10 seem to suggest the V chord (F) with the root (F), 4th (B♭), and ♭7th (E♭) notes, while in measures 11–13, where Johnson lays out vocally, his "blues machine" does the talking (in the key of A) with the strongest scale degrees: root (A), 3rd (C♯), 5th (E), and ♭7th (G).

Note: As mentioned in the intro, in measure 45 (verse 4), Johnson certainly appears to be referencing the V chord with his guitar and vocal.

**Come on in
My Kitchen
Example 2**

With the former, he plays D/B (♭7th/5th) and string 6 (E) open. With the latter, he sustains E♭, the ♭7th of F (V chord in the key of B♭).

Bridge

The bridge contains a startling sound effect in measures 33–34 (similarly in measures 35–36), where Johnson imitates the wind howling.

Come on in
My Kitchen
Example 3

*Slide positioned halfway between 14th and 15th frets.

Observe how he steps outside the diatonic key of A with microtones between frets 14 and 15 and frets 11 and 12 before resolving to the tonic note (A).

Verse 5

The last measure of the song is an uplifting end on the tonic chord, delivered with a tender touch. Johnson combines A (root), G (♭7th), A, E (5th), C♯/A (3rd/root), and E (octave) notes without the slide before concluding with a sweetly vibratoed A (octave) with the slide, leaving the last note hanging in the air.

Come on in
My Kitchen
Example 4

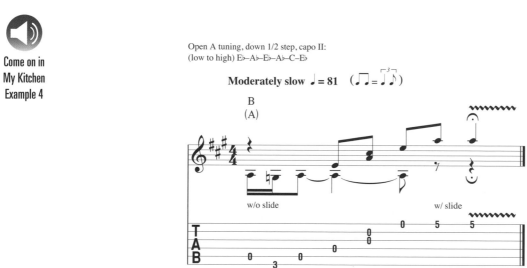

COME ON IN MY KITCHEN

Words and Music by Robert Johnson

Come on in
My Kitchen
Full Song

* Open A tuning, down 1/2 step, capo II:
(low to high) E♭–A♭–E♭–A♭–C–E♭

****Symbols in parentheses represent chord names (implied harmony) respective to capoed guitar.
Symbols above reflect harmony implied by vocals. Capoed fret is "0" in tab.
***Downstemmed notes only.**

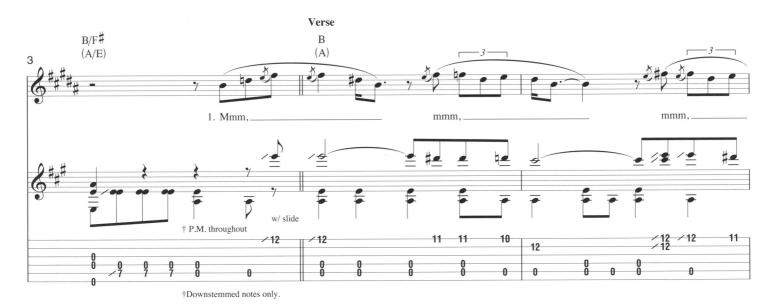

†Downstemmed notes only.

*Tunings were determined using the original 78s.

4. When a wom-an gets in trou-ble,_____ ev-'ry-bod-y throws her down._

Look-in' for her good friend, none can_ be found. You bet-ter come

on in my kitch-en. Ba-by, it's gon' to be rain-in' out-doors._

5. Win-ter time's com-

*Upstemmed notes only.

Cross Road Blues (Crossroads)
Recorded Friday, November 27, 1936, in San Antonio, Texas

"Cross Road Blues," often referred to as just "Crossroads," has been covered many times, most notably by virtuosic blues-rocker Eric Clapton while in Cream. This song is also one element in the unstoppable myth, among rock fans particularly, that Johnson sold his soul to the devil for his remarkable instrumental virtuosity. In reality, it is a dynamic, dramatically syncopated blues standard showing exceptional finger and vocal independence, as Johnson's voice glides effortlessly over top of his aggressive yet legato phrasing. w/o slide

Intro

The four-measure intro is another Johnson classic. In measures 1 and 2, he establishes his A tonality with the slide. In measures 3 and 4, without the slide, he walks down the fretboard, implying the I (A7/G), IV (D/F♯), iv (Dm/F), I (A/E), and V (E7) changes. Of interest is his use of octaves on the E strings (6 and 4), which he gave a passing nod to in "Come on in My Kitchen," but here, he hits them prominently on beats 2, 3, and 4.

Crossroads
Example 1

Open A tuning, down 1/2 step, capo II:
(low to high) E♭–A♭–E♭–A♭–C–E♭

*Symbols in parentheses represent chord names (implied harmony) respective to capoed guitar.
Symbols above reflect harmony implied by vocals. Capoed fret is "0" in tab.

Performance Tip: Use the thumb on string 6 and the index finger strumming upward on strings 3 and 4 simultaneously. Or, utilize the index for string 4 and the middle finger for string 3.

Verse 1

Verses 1 and 4 have 15 measures each, but the former begins with six measures of the I chord (A) and ends with two measures of the I, whereas verse 4 starts with five measures of the I chord and concludes with four measures of the I. Verses 2 and 3 have exactly the same 14 measures. Take note how the verses end on the I chord, rather than resolving to the V chord (E), in order to keep the momentum going.

Beginning in Verse 1, Johnson employs "call and response" to great effect. His arrangement is to sing for roughly two measures and then fill instrumentally for two or three. The result is quite hypnotic. Of paramount importance is the way he indicates the I, IV, and V changes with the slide by isolating mostly dyads. Measures 5–10 are an excellent indication of his intelligent choices.

Crossroads
Example 2

Open A tuning, down 1/2 step, capo II:
(low to high) Eb–Ab–Eb–Ab–C–Eb

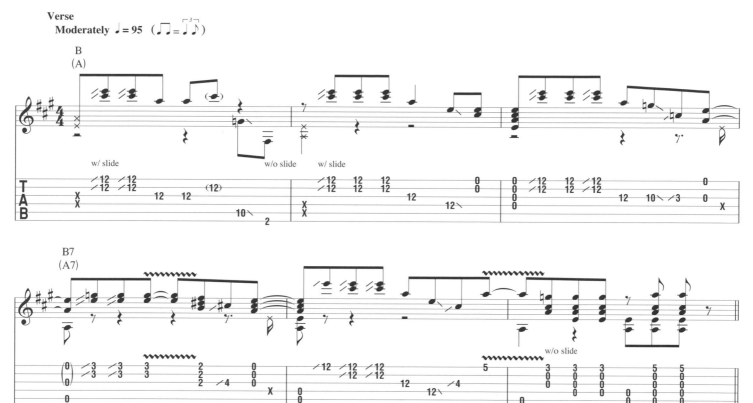

In measures 5, 6, 7, and 9, Johnson emphasizes E/C♯ (5th/3rd) for the I chord (A), while in measure 8, he implies a vibrant A7 dyad, G/E (♭7th/5th), on beats 1 and 2. Observe the quick "hit" on beat 3 of measure 8, where he plays an F♯/D♯/B (6th/♯4th/9th) "grace chord" on the way back to A major, sustaining an A major triad E/C♯/A (5th/3rd/root) across the bar line, into measure 9. In measure 10, however, Johnson fingers A7 and A major with big, dynamic, resonant voicings sans the slide.

In open A tuning (as well as in open G, open D, and open E tunings), the main harmony for the IV chord resides conveniently at fret 5. Measures 11–12 contain the D major triad A/F♯/D (5th/3rd/root), along with C/A/A (♭7th/5th/5th) and related dyads to imply D7, which Johnson fingers in a highly syncopated and distinctive manner as one of the signature motifs of the track.

Performance Tip: Use a combination of the index and ring fingers as partial barres.

Measures 13–15 (I chord, A) function as the instrumental "response" to the vocal "call" in measures 11–12. As in measures 5–10, Johnson dynamically follows slide riffs with fretted A and A7 voicings.

Performance Tip: The fretted major and seventh chord voicings in open A are a staple of Delta blues guitar to be employed as desired. Observe how the open-string voicings can be converted to moveable closed IV (D) and V (E) chords.

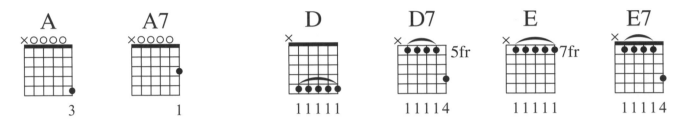

One of the nuances of blues guitar that separates the real "funk" from the "deodorized" variety of America's "classical music," are the quarter-step bends to the true blue notes between the ♭3rd and major 3rd and ♭7th and major 7th degrees. Check out measure 14 (I chord, A), where Johnson singles out the C (♭3rd) on string 3 and bends it a quarter step.

Crossroads Example 4

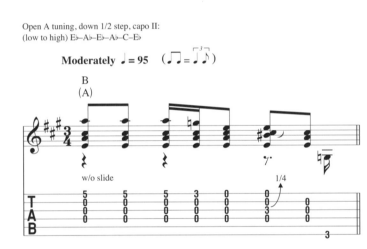

A more common blues guitar bend is a half step from the ♭3rd to the major 3rd, as seen in measure 18.

Crossroads Example 5

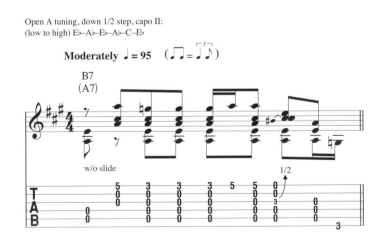

Both bends are telling instances of his attention to detail, contributing to the overall pungent aroma of real country blues!

CROSS ROAD BLUES (CROSSROADS)

Words and Music by Robert Johnson

Crossroads
Full Song

* Open A tuning, down 1/2 step, capo II:
(low to high) E♭–A♭–E♭–A♭–C–E♭

**Symbols in parentheses represent chord names (implied harmony) respective to capoed guitar.
Symbols above reflect harmony implied by vocals. Capoed fret is "0" in tab.

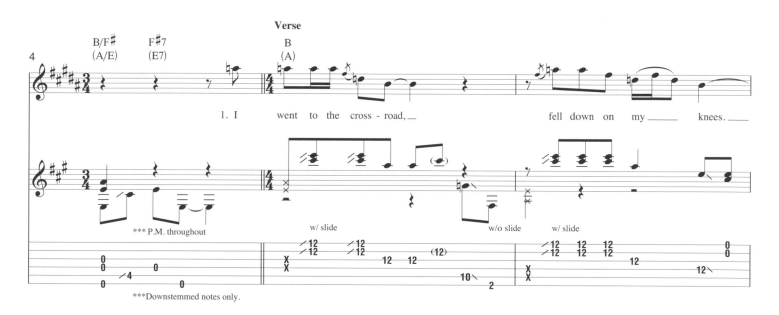

***Downstemmed notes only.

*Tunings were determined using the original 78s.

I went to the cross - road,

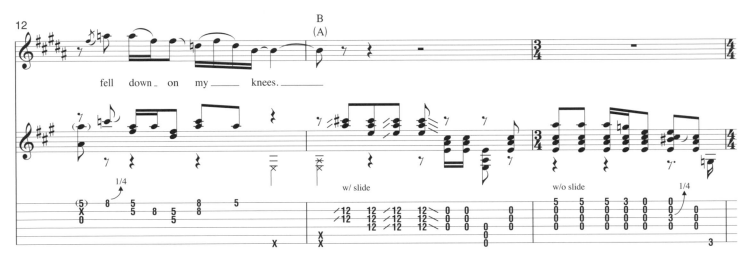

fell down on my knees.

Asked the Lord a - bove, "Have mer - cy.

Save poor Bob, if you please."

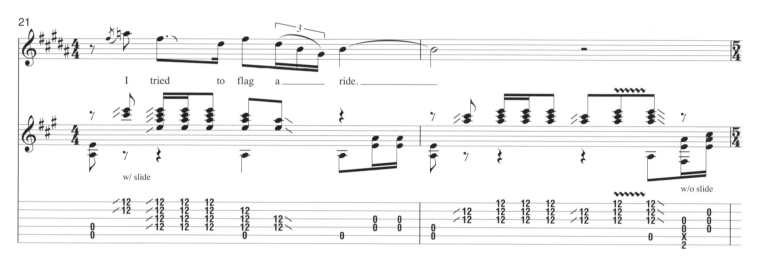

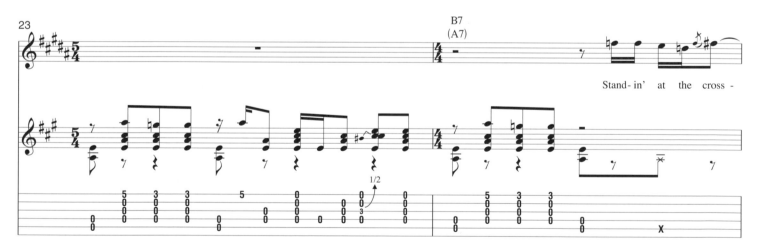

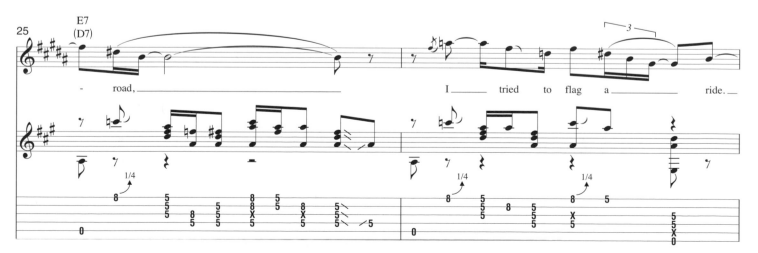

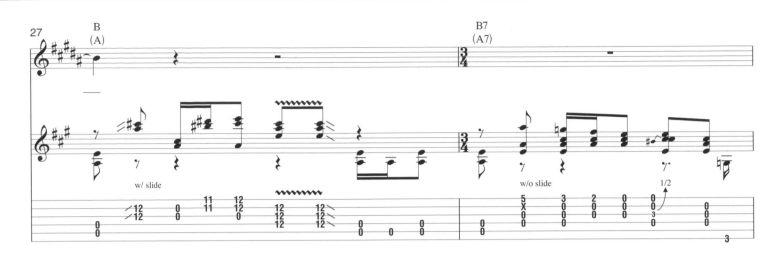

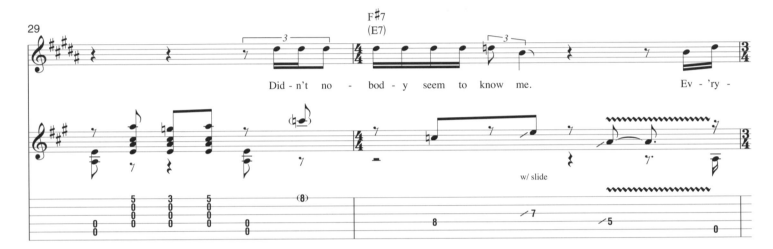

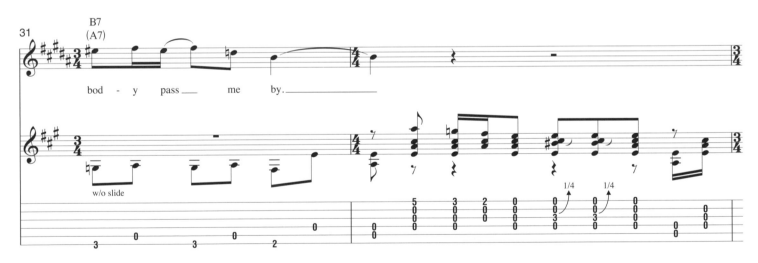

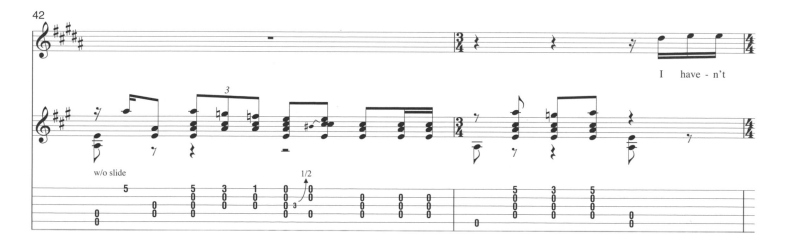

got no lov - in' sweet wom - an that ___ love and feel my care. ___

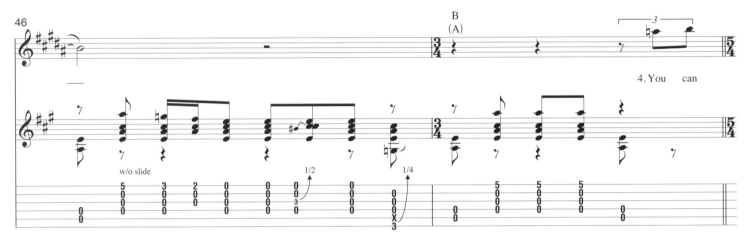

___ 4. You can

Verse

run, you can run. ___ Tell my friend-boy Wil-lie Brown. ___

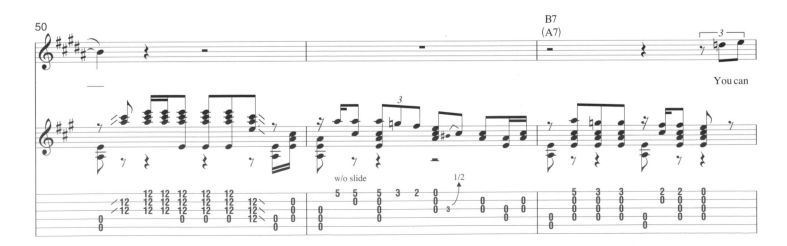

You can

run,_____ tell my friend - boy Wil - lie Brown._____

Lord, that I'm

stand - in' at the cross - road, babe, I be - lieve I'm sink - in' down.____

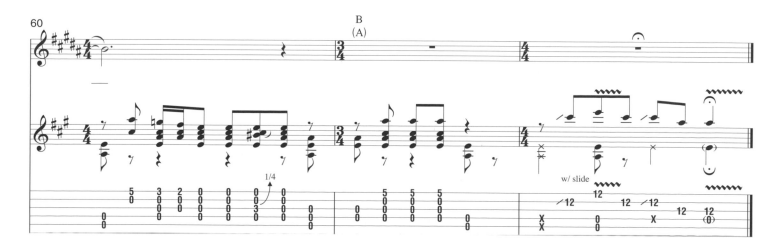

ESSENTIAL LICKS

Boogie Patterns

Robert Johnson was not the first to record boogie patterns. More correctly termed "cut boogie," as they are essentially a truncated version of walking piano boogie-woogie bass lines, they were initially waxed by Johnny Temple in 1935 on "Lead Pencil Blues."

Performance Tip: Like Johnson's "Phonograph Blues," "Lead Pencil Blues" euphemistically refers to a bout of impotence.

Though containing virtually the same accompaniment as found in "Sweet Home Chicago," "When You Got a Good Friend" shows how Johnson incorporated open strings to a greater degree in order to fatten up the basic bass-string harmony of 5ths and 6ths and, in the case of the IV chord (A), the ♭7th.

Lick 1

In this first lick, Johnson displays knowledge of the fingerboard beyond the scope of most, if not all, of his peers. After plucking strings 6 and 5 open on the downbeat of beat 4, he jumps to fret 9 for a slick, sweet C♯/E (6th/root) dyad, played in conjunction with the same open strings on the upbeat of beat 4. No wonder "Keef" thought there were two guitarists playing when he first heard the recordings!

Lick 2

Over the I chord (A) in measure 1 of verse 1 of "I'm a Steady Rollin' Man," Johnson adds the classic bass-string embellishment of the ♭3rd (C) to the major 3rd (C♯) on beat 4. Though not the first to utilize the blues-approved move, his prominent usage of it in several songs likely influenced countless other blues guitarists, peers, and followers.

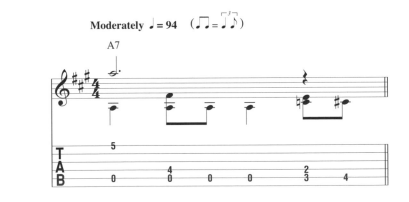

Lick 3

Over the I chord in measure 1 of verse 5 of "I'm a Steady Rollin' Man," Johnson inserts what is essentially a first-inversion A major triad with the 3rd (C♯) on the bottom. What makes it even more significant is the way it's combined with the ♭3rd–♮3rd embellishment in a lick so cool a whole song could be based around it.

Performance Tip: Access the A/E notes with the index finger. It should be a snap, as the index finger is already on string 4 on beats 1 and 2.

Lick 3

Lick 4

Open E tuning, like open D, contains the same relationship of 5ths between strings 6 and 5. Hence, bass-string boogie patterns in 5ths, 6ths, and even ♭7ths fall easily under the fingers. In open E, "Ramblin' on My Mind" is the only Robert Johnson composition that combines slide riffs and boogie patterns, with most of the latter employed similarly to standard tuning. However, check out measures 6–7 of verse 3, where he connects the I chord (E) to the IV chord (A) with an almost totally chromatic walk up the bass strings in 5ths: F♯5 (F♯/C♯), G5 (G/D), and G♯5 (G♯/D♯). Additionally, he avoids the expected resolution to E/A at fret 5 on the downbeat of measure 7, instead playing a fretted A note over the open fifth string (B), adding the open first string (E) for "good measure."

Lick 4

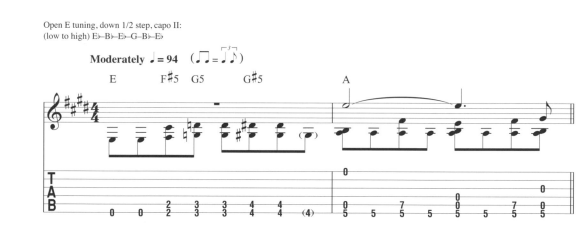

Lick 5

When studying bass-string boogie patterns, subtle variations are often the rule rather than the exception. In measure 9 of verse 5 of "Ramblin' on My Mind," Johnson throws in a quick A voicing on beat 4 for a quick IV chord reference.

Performance Tip: Assuming the middle finger will have been playing the C♯ note on fret 2 of string 5, it is an easy move to add the A on fret 1 of string 3 in conjunction with the open fourth string (E) to complete the major chord.

Lick 5

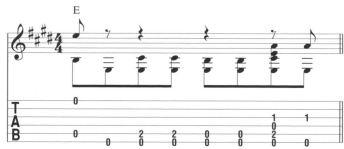

Lick 6

Though not specifically a Robert Johnson *essential* lick, his method of playing the V chord (B) in "Ramblin'" can be a valuable musical tool when playing in open E or open D, for example. With string 5 tuned to B, the 5th of the key of E (and root of the V chord), it is a cinch to play the cut boogie pattern as if it is the E (I chord) change. Incidentally, Jimmy Reed used to do the same thing in standard tuning, with string 5 tuned to A. The result is that the A string functions as the ♭7th of the B (V chord) and sounds fine when combined with a bass playing the root (B) or another guitarist playing a B boogie pattern with the root on the bottom.

Lick 6

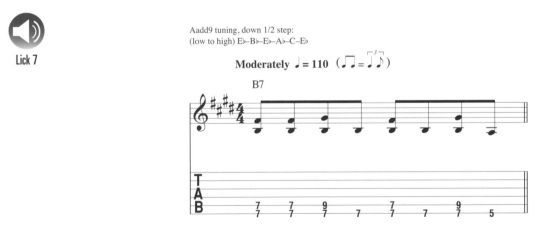

Lick 7

When in Aadd9 tuning, over the V chord (B), Johnson opts for the more common technique when string 5 is tuned up to B: he just barres fret 7 on the two bottom bass strings.

Performance Tip: Barre with the index finger and use the ring finger to add the 6th on string 5. By the way, the same pattern and fingering is utilized for the IV chord (A), only two frets lower, and can be applied to other songs with the same relative tuning on the two bottom bass strings.

Lick 7

Diminished Seventh Chords

Johnson consistently incorporated diminished seventh chords into riffs and licks.

Lick 8

Though not the first prewar blues guitarist to employ diminished seventh chords, with Lonnie Johnson prominently preceding him, Robert notably presented them in several of his most well-known compositions, beginning with "Kind Hearted Woman Blues." In measures 1 and 2 of verse 1, he plays a hip A7 (I7) voicing in the former and a hip A°7 (I°7) voicing in the latter. Both are voiced in the fifth position and make use of the open fifth string.

Performance Tip: Following a I or I7 chord with a I°7 is a way of breaking up a "slow change," which typically contains I7 voicings in measures 1–4 of a 12-bar blues.

Lick 8

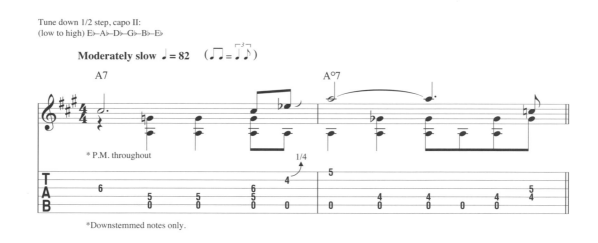

Lick 9

Measure 4 of verse 2 in "Kind Hearted Woman Blues" shows Johnson moving from A7 to A°7 and back to A7 within the span of one measure. Take note of the way he combines strummed voicings and single notes in triplet phrasing via arpeggiation.

Lick 9

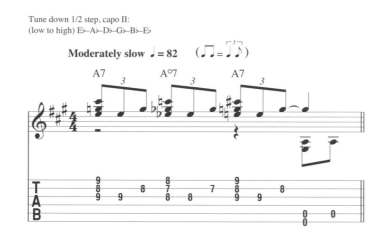

Lick 10

In this lick, Johnson emphasizes the lower strings as he moves from A7 to A°7 and then resolves back to A7 in measure 8. The moves produce a gritty "growl," as well as dynamic contrast to the implied trebly A major on strings 3–1 (measure 8).

Lick 10

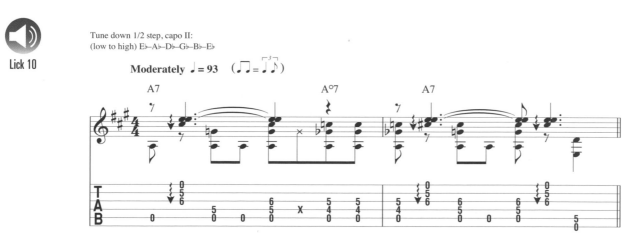

Lick 11

In measures 1–3 (I chord) of verse 6 in "32–20 Blues," an unusual chord move for Delta blues guitarists appears, as Johnson opts for A–Am7–A rather than his "patented" A7–A°7–A7. Nevertheless, this sequence is a worthy substitute.

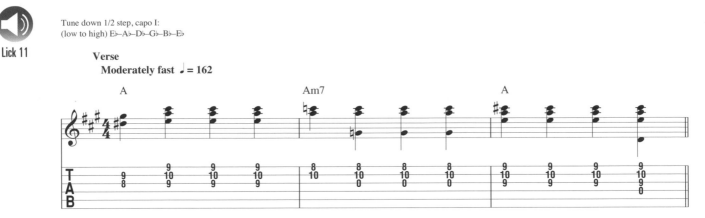

Standard-Tuned Chord Voicings

Though not really "licks," the following chord shapes highlight some of Johnson's common grips.

Lick 12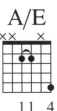

A pertinent characteristic of Robert Johnson's technique is his use of "edited" chord voicings. The second inversion (5th on bottom) A major chord here contains only E, A, and A (octave) but makes for logical resolution following his typical turnaround pattern with the descending notes on string 4.

Performance Tip: Pluck the chord with the right-hand thumb on string 4, index on string 3, and ring on string 1.

Lick 13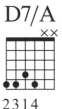

A big, fat second-inversion D7 functioning as the IV chord makes its appearance in "Kind Hearted Woman Blues."

Lick 14

Perhaps too obvious, but the implied bass-string E7 that appears in "Sweet Home Chicago" and elsewhere shows how Johnson could say a lot with very little. Played open, strings 6 (E) and 4 (D) create a bluesy rumble.

Lick 15

Another E7 voicing seen in the turnaround of "Sweet Home Chicago," this E7/B chord is played on the top three strings. Johnson arpeggiates the chord, and don't overlook the open first string (E), an important technique in Delta blues guitar.

Lick 16

An exceedingly cool A7 voicing is found in "Kind Hearted Woman Blues" and its "sister" tune, "Phonograph Blues."

Performance Tip: This voicing is moveable to other frets/chords if the open high E string is avoided.

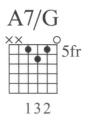

Standard-Tuned Licks

Lick 17

Colloquially known as the blues "train whistle," the double-stop lick shown in "Sweet Home Chicago" is a classic known and beloved by virtually all blues guitarists.

Performance Tip: Be sure to bend string 2 up a quarter step—not a full half step—unless the desire is to produce a harmonious B/G♯ (5th/3rd) dyad implying E major instead of funky blues dissonance (see photo).

Lick 17

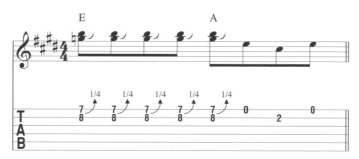

Lick 18

Johnson liked to move from A major, barred at the second position with string 5 open and the A note on string 1 fretted at fret 5, to A7 at the second position via the addition of G (♭7th) on fret 3 of string 1. Throughout "Steady Rollin' Man," he embellishes the classic blues harmony of the I chord through a combination of triplets and swung eighth-note phrasing, as seen most clearly in measures 3 and 4 of verse 1.

Performance Tip: Use the left-hand pinky for the high A note (fret 5) and the middle finger for the G note (fret 3) on string 1.

Lick 18

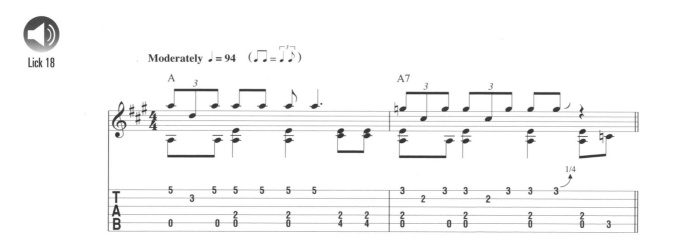

Lick 19

Similar to a verse lick in Johnson's "Little Queen of Spades," he employs his signature turnaround, descending *and* ascending, over the I (A) chord as a full-bodied chordal fill operating in contrast to the sparse forms of the other measures.

Performance Tip: Dig how the A7 triple-stop voicing on strings 3–1 at fret 9 transforms into A°7 and Dm6 when lowered to frets 8 and 7, respectively.

Lick 19

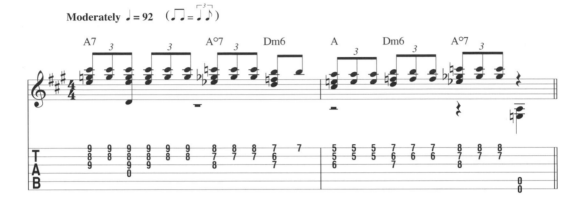

Lick 20

Here's yet another variation on A7–A°7–A7.

Performance Tip: Set the fret hand on the A7/G voicing as first seen in "Kind Hearted Woman Blues," with the index on string 4 at fret 5 (G), the ring finger on string 3 at fret 6 (C♯), and the middle finger on string 2 at fret 5 (E). Pick the appropriate strings as indicated, moving the left hand down the fingerboard one fret for the A°7 chord on beat 4 of the first measure.

Lick 20

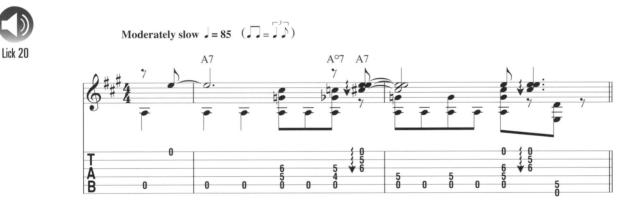

Lick 21

Johnson could pack more cool blues guitar info into one measure than some guitarists could into an entire verse, as heard in this embellished A7 chord change. Though it is only one note out of a triplet, the E♭ (♭5th) on beat 3 is perfectly placed for maximum true-blues tonality.

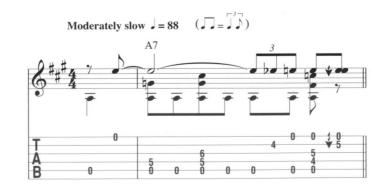

Lick 21

Lick 22

This lick in the style of "Honeymoon Blues" shows even more advanced Delta blues brilliance. From A7–E7–A7 changes, Johnson creates a flowing succession of choice dyads and steady bass-string accompaniment.

Performance Tip: In measure 2, barre strings 2 and 1 at fret 2 with your index finger, using your pinky and middle fingers to access the A and G notes on string 1, respectively.

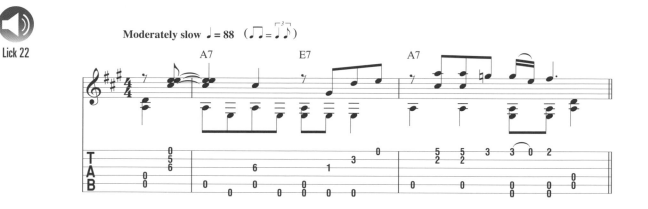

Slide Licks

Note: As far as what is known, Johnson never recorded slide in standard tuning like his running buddy, the late Honeyboy Edwards. In addition, he rarely embellished his slide licks with much vibrato, perhaps because there was so much else to occupy his fingers as a solo acoustic guitarist!

Lick 23

In measures 1–4 of the bridge (I chord, A) in "Come on in My Kitchen," played in open A, Johnson conjures up the sound of the wind howling via the creative and skillful manipulation of his slider above the octave. Of particular note is the way he positions it between frets 14 and 15 and 11 and 12, respectively.

Performance Tip: Be aware that the placement of the slider for the in-between microtones is more of a feel thing than a prescription for exact intonation.

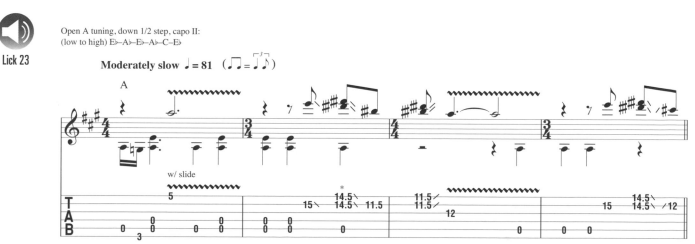

*Slide positioned halfway between 14th and 15th frets.

Lick 24

Measure 1 of the intro (I chord, A) in "Terraplane Blues," played in open A, contains an instructive slide figure with dyads and one triad. E/C# (5th/3rd), E/C#/A (5th/3rd/root), G/E (♭7th/5th), and F#/D# (6th/#4th), followed by string 2 (C#) open, leads logically and smoothly to the A7 chord change in measure 2 (not shown).

Lick 24

Lick 25

Measures 1–2 of the intro (I chord, A) to "Cross Road Blues," played in open A, combine the classic E/C# dyad and the choice single notes of C# (3rd), A (root), C (♭3rd), A (lower octave), and A (octave above). Conclusively nailing the I chord tonality, Johnson follows this with one of his favorite descending turnaround patterns, played with the fingers, of course (not shown).

Lick 25

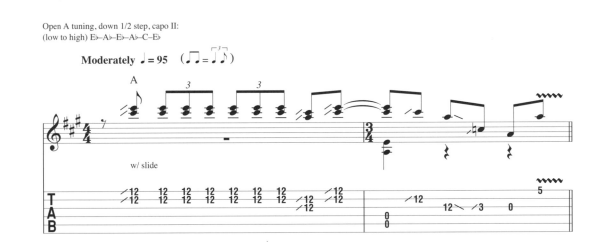

Lick 26

In measures 1–4 of verse 1 in "Walkin' Blues," played in open A, Johnson employs his slider in the most minimal but effective way to embellish his "walking," stomping blues. The ♭3rd (C) to ♮3rd (C#) bass lick is as characteristic of the blues as a catfish and a train whistle.

Lick 26

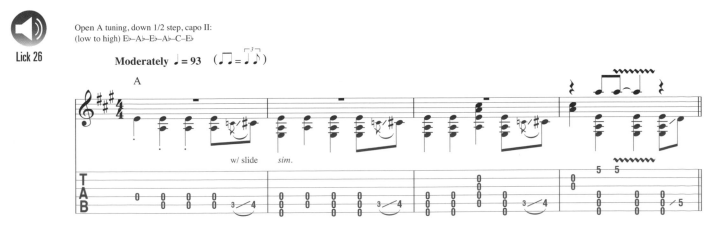

Lick 27

Johnson took a musical page from the "Rollin' and Tumblin'" playbook and crafted his own memorable version of a signature lick by combining the open strings A/E/A (root/5th/root) and the major triad E/C♯/A (5th/3rd/root) with the grainy triple stop G/E/C (♭7th/5th/♭3rd) and a slick G♯ (major 7th) octave jump.

Performance Tip: As is often the case with Johnson's slide tunes, it is necessary to pay close attention to fretted notes and slide notes, which often alternate quickly.

Lick 27

Lick 28

For those who believe playing notated slide beyond the end of the fingerboard was a much later invention by, say, the great Duane Allman, for example, this lick will kick that idea to the curb. Starting over the imaginary 25th fret (F/D = ♭6th/4th), he continues his way back down with equally nasty-sounding dyads over "frets" 23 (E♭/C = ♭5th/♭3rd), 22 (D/B = 4th/9th), and 20 (C/A = ♭3rd/root) until he returns to *terra firma* over fret 17 (A = root), fret 14 (F♯/D♯ = 6th/♯4th), and fret 10 (D/B = 4th/9th).

Performance Tip: Clearly, playing slide past the end of the fingerboard is a "feel thing" requiring a finely tuned ear. So, go for it!

Lick 28

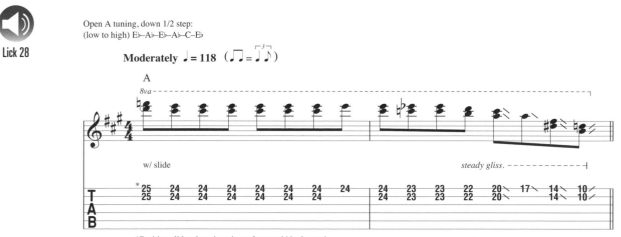

*Position slide where imaginary fret would be located.

Lick 29

One of the many reasons Keith Richards, on his initial listening to Robert Johnson, probably thought there were two guitarists playing may be heard in tunes like "Traveling Riverside Blues," and others. Showing his unexcelled skill at weaving syncopated open strings and fretted bass-string notes with slide licks, he throws down the gauntlet to would-be Delta bluesmen everywhere.

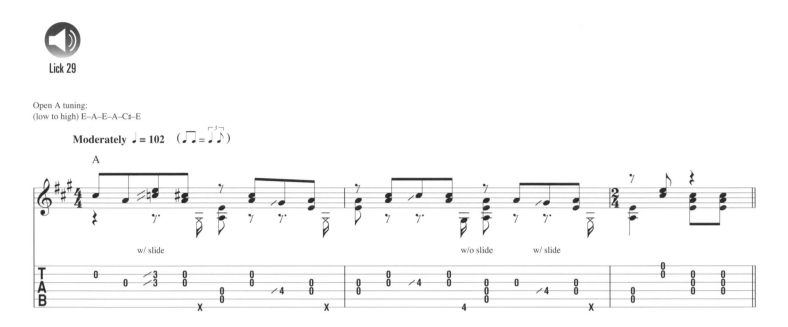

Lick 30

At his final recording session, Johnson created an intro like none of his others, perhaps pointing in a new direction in which he was about to embark. In this similar passage, following the pickup notes A and B♭ over the V chord (E7) in measure 1, he plays A (4th), G♯ (3rd), B/G♯ (5th/3rd), E (root), and A. In measure 2, over the IV chord (D7), he picks C/A (♭7th/5th), E (2nd), G/E (4th/2nd), F♯/D♯ (3rd/♭2nd), and C♯ (major 7th), which precedes the open third string, A. The proliferation of tart, altered tones contributes to a sophisticated, melancholy blues melody not previously heard in his music.

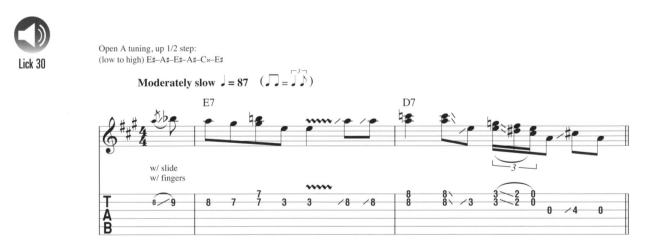

SIGNATURE RIFFS

Ramblin' on My Mind
Recorded Monday, November 23, 1936, in San Antonio, Texas

As previously noted in Lick 4 of Essential Licks, "Ramblin' on My Mind," played in open E, is the only Johnson song combining boogie bass-string patterns with slide. At the same time, it resembles the standard-tuned "Sweet Home Chicago" in rhythmic feel and phrasing. Popular versions of "M & O Blues" by pianists Walter Davis and Roosevelt Sykes were likely inspirations. Eric Clapton sang and played a simplified version in standard tuning without slide on *John Mayall & the Bluesbreakers featuring Eric Clapton* in 1966.

Intro

Delivering one of his famed "double turnarounds" in measures 1–5 of the intro, Johnson combines slithery slide licks and fretted notes in a remarkable template for future blues guitarists and countless other compositions. Do not miss the cool, bluesy nuance in measure 2, where he inserts the C (♭6th, or hip ♯5th) in between the typical boogie dyads of a 5th (B/E) and a 6th (C♯/E). Even more important, pay close attention to measures 1 and 3, where he simultaneously plays slide licks on the upper strings while thumping on the open sixth (E) and fifth (B) strings!

Performance Tip 1: In measures 1 and 3, be sure to carefully lay the slide on strings 3–1 only, picking the notes with the index or the index and the middle fingers while bumping the open bass strings with the thumb.

Performance Tip 2: On beat 4 of measure 3, notice the rare expression of vibrato on the root (E) on fret 12 of string 1, sustained into measure 4.

Ramblin'
Intro

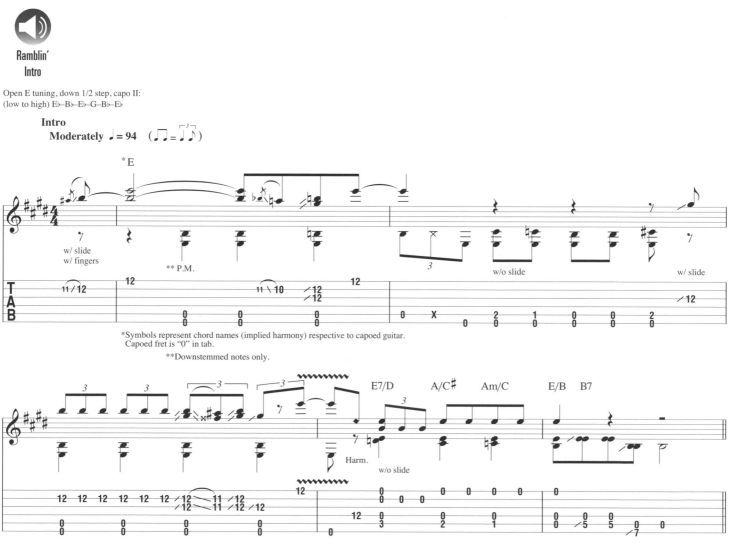

Open E tuning, down 1/2 step, capo II:
(low to high) E♭–B♭–E♭–G–B♭–E♭

Intro
Moderately ♩ = 94

*Symbols represent chord names (implied harmony) respective to capoed guitar.
Capoed fret is "0" in tab.
**Downstemmed notes only.

Verse 2

The "standard" 12-bar blues with the "slow change" occasionally finds Johnson stretching some measures to five or six quarter-note beats. Verse 2, however, is in regular 4/4 time throughout, and it is recommended that all verses be performed as such. As seen previously in Lick 6 of Essential Licks, Johnson smartly and efficiently plays the V chord (B) in measure 9 by taking advantage of string 5 being tuned up to B instead of playing it at fret 7, in a manner similar to the IV chord (A) at fret 5. Observe how Johnson only slides in measures 1–3 (I chord) as melodic accompaniment to his vocals.

Ramblin'
Verse 2

Open E tuning, down 1/2 step, capo II:
(low to high) E♭–B♭–E♭–G–B♭–E♭

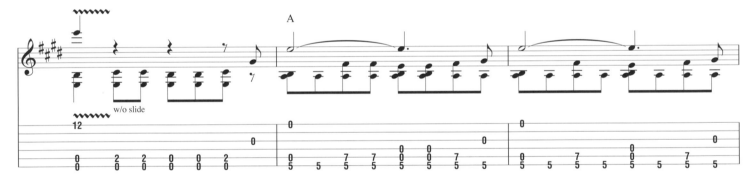

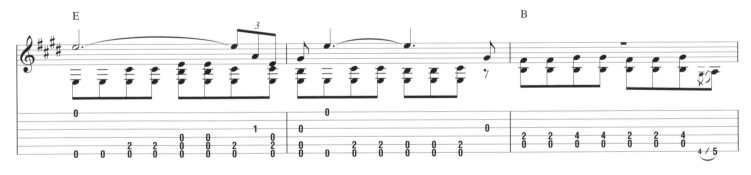

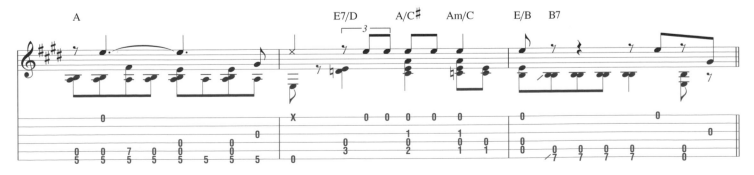

Terraplane Blues
Recorded Monday, November 23, 1936, in San Antonio, Texas

A "Terraplane" was a budget-priced, speedy automobile made by the Hudson Motor Car Company in Detroit from 1932–36. However, Johnson had no interest in extolling the virtues of a popular vehicle, but instead using it as a witty, sexual metaphor. In turn, "Terraplane Blues" b/w "Kind Hearted Woman Blues" became his most popular and requested recording, reportedly selling a then-hefty 5,000 copies. Although perhaps apocryphal, there is the story of a young lady hearing the record played in his presence. When Johnson informed her that he was the artist, she refused to believe him until he got his guitar and performed it for her.

Intro

Though he announces his considerable presence with slyly insistent open-A slide licks in measure 1 of the intro, the body of the song contains mostly fretted chordal riffs. Observe the slimmed-down turnaround pattern on the middle strings in measure 2, which harmonizes only with A7 and does not resolve to the V chord (E) or, in fact, "turn around." Equally unique is measure 3, which, for all practical purposes, functions as the first measure of verse 1, as it is similar to the verse riffs in phrasing and harmony.

Performance Tip: The way Johnson moves in measure 1 from E/C♯ (5th/3rd) to G/E (♭7th/5th), F♯/D♯ (6th/♯4th), and C♯ (3rd) is as smooth as that old Hudson rolling down Highway 61.

Terraplane Blues
Intro

Open A tuning, down 1/2 step, capo II:
(low to high) E♭–A♭–E♭–A♭–C–E♭

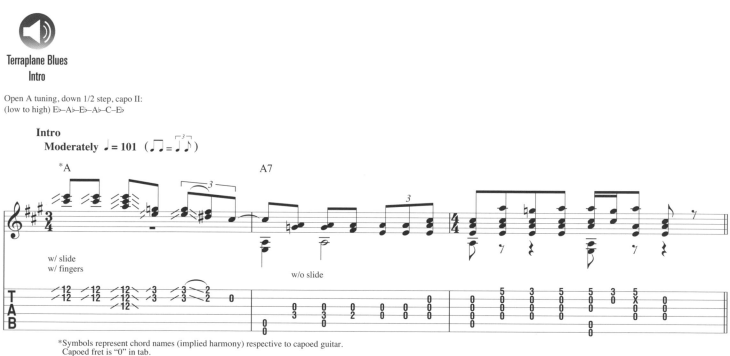

*Symbols represent chord names (implied harmony) respective to capoed guitar.
Capoed fret is "0" in tab.

Verse 3

Along with some of his most suggestive lyrics, Johnson continues to smack his strings with lusty abandon and salacious dynamic syncopation. Check out measures 5 and 6 (IV chord, D7), where he plays the most minimal slide licks with the C (♭7th) and A (5th) notes to imply the D7 harmony. Likewise, he does a similar thing in measures 9 and 10 (V and IV chords, respectively). The effect is dramatic and allows his romantic entreaties to stand out.

Terraplane Blues
Verse 3

Open A tuning, down 1/2 step, capo II:
(low to high) E♭–A♭–E♭–A♭–C–E♭

Verse
Moderately ♩ = 101 (♫ = ♪)

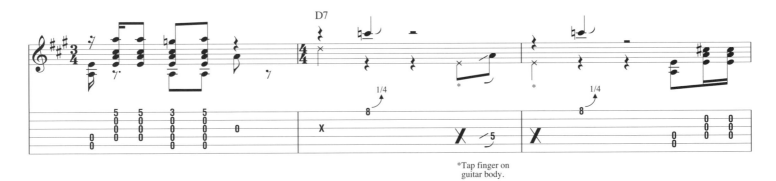

*Tap finger on
guitar body.

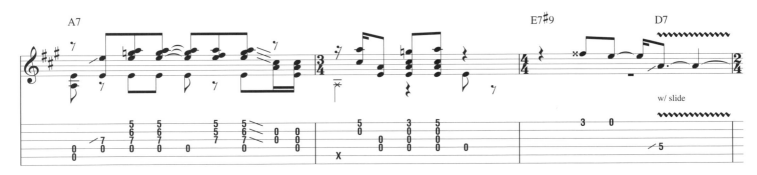

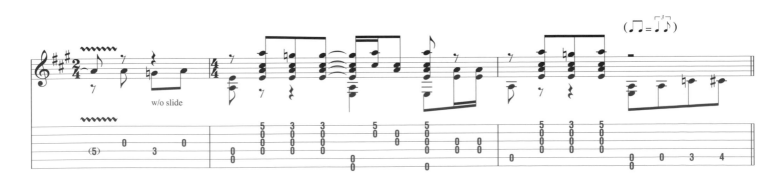

Bridge

Johnson "switches gears" to a boogie shuffle in measures 1–4 (I chord) of the bridge, driven by the classic A (root), C (♭3rd), and C♯ (major 3rd) bass line. Johnson obviously delights in inventing more and more metaphors for body parts as he goes along, reaching a "climax" of sorts in measure 7 (I chord), where he stomps down hard with his slide at fret 12, the A octave. Similar to verse 3, he "throttles back" with choice slide and fretted notes in measures 9 and 10.

Terraplane Blues
Bridge

Open A tuning, down 1/2 step, capo II:
(low to high) E♭–A♭–E♭–A♭–C–E♭

Bridge
Moderately ♩ = 101

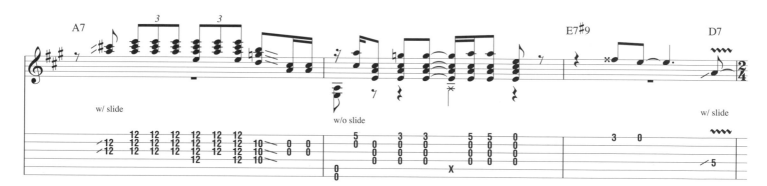

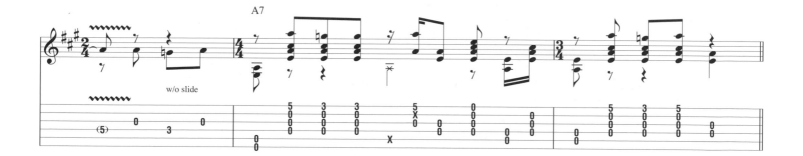

32–20 Blues
Recorded Thursday, November 26, 1936, in San Antonio, Texas

Taking lyrical and musical inspiration, to a degree, from Skip James' "22–20 Blues" and his title from Roosevelt Sykes' "32–20 Blues," both piano pieces, Johnson invented a rockin' version all his own. It is as near virtuosic as "Preachin' Blues," with steady, independent bass-string-powered propulsion implied, if not literally played, in every measure as another instance of his technical skill of sounding like two guitarists. Though not shown, verse 1, at 13 measures long, has an extra measure of A°, which is likely a mistake, perhaps due to his nervousness at the recording session for this one song.

Intro

With his thumb as a musical piston, Johnson sets the groove with steady quarter notes, save for beat 1 in measure 1, where he sustains C♯/G (3rd/♭7th) the length of the measure while he pounds quarter notes on beats 2–4. The result drives his "double turnaround" without letup, right into verse 1 (not shown).

Performance Tip: In measures 3 and 4, lock in the index finger as a barre at fret 2 while utilizing the other three fingers logically to access the additional notes.

32–20 Blues
Intro

*Symbols represent chord names (implied harmony) respective to capoed guitar.
Capoed fret is "0" in tab.
**Downstemmed notes only.

Verse 4

Verse 4 is one the best-performed verses on the recording, which sometimes finds Johnson struggling a bit to fit his lyrics in the standard 12-bar form that he sets for himself. Hence, verse 4 is a 12-bar blues with 12 measures in 4/4 time, with no measures in 2/4 time.

Performance Tip: As technically precise as it is, the B♭ note on beat 1 of measure 4 (I chord, A7) is questionable, though it goes by in a blink of the eye.

32–20 Blues
Verse 4

Tune down 1/2 step, capo I:
(low to high) E♭–A♭–D♭–G♭–B♭–E♭

Verse
Moderately fast ♩ = 162

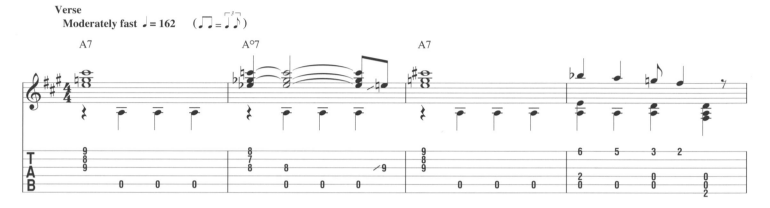

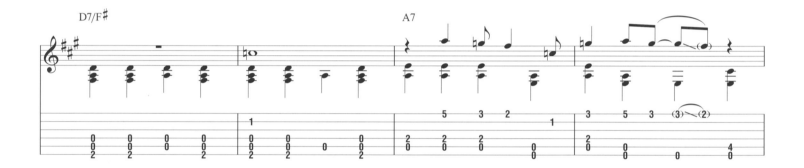

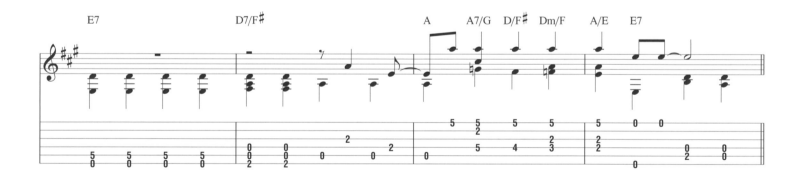

Verse 10

Johnson swings his comping in measures 1–3 and 5–6 of verse 10 like a blues-breaking Freddie Green. Similar to verse 4, he also grooves smoothly throughout. The turnaround in measures 11–12 is the same as the one used in the intro and verse 4, only he lands on a slick A7 chord featuring the ♭7th on fret 3 of string 1 to bring the song to a dramatic conclusion.

Performance Tip: Use the middle finger for the ♭7th note of the A7 chord, with an index-finger barre handling the other notes.

32–20 Blues
Verse 10

Tune down 1/2 step, capo I:
(low to high) E♭–A♭–D♭–G♭–B♭–E♭

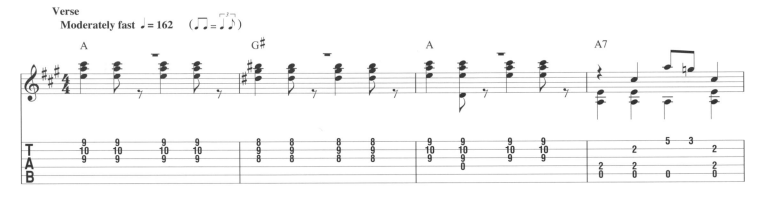

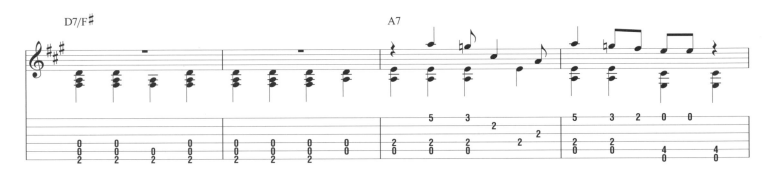

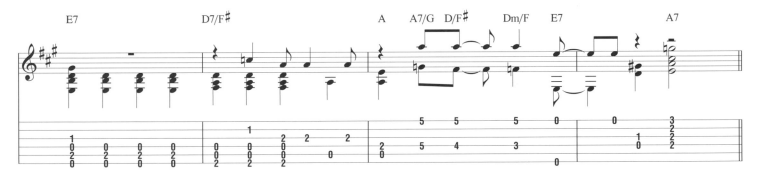

They're Red Hot
Recorded Friday, November 26, 1936, in San Antonio, Texas

An often-overlooked subgenre of prewar blues is the humorous "hokum music." Legendary prewar bands like the Mississippi Sheiks, Gus Cannon's Jug Stompers, and Will Shade's Memphis Jug Band played blues, as well as hokum. Growing out of minstrelsy, the style typically found its humor in sexual innuendo and double entendres. The great blues guitarists Tampa Red and Big Bill Broonzy had plied their trade in hokum bands, and Johnson decided to add his name to the list. His take on the style was influenced by Tampa Red's "What Is It That Tastes Like Gravy" from 1929, albeit "cleaned up."

Intro

The two-measure intro in the "people's key" of C begins on the tonic, moving through a cycle of 4ths—D7, G7 (G), C, and F (Fm)—before resolving to the V chord (G7). Adding to the natural pull of "gravity" created by the descending triad and triple-stop voicings on the top three strings in measure 1 is the dynamic drop in register Johnson presents in measure 2.

Performance Tip: Playing full-bodied solo blues guitar, or any genre for that matter, seems to require steady bass figures and bottom-heavy voicings for a full sound. However, well-chosen triads and triple stops on the top strings, when strummed with authority, can also drive a progression with power. In that regard, use crisp downstrokes throughout, like a swing jazz guitarist from the '30s and '40s.

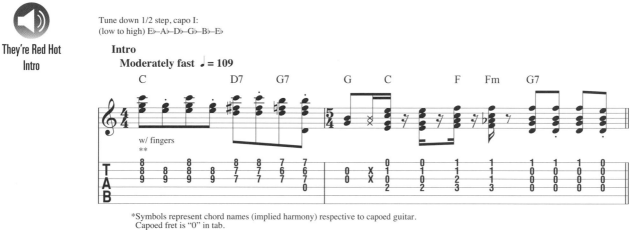

They're Red Hot
Intro

*Symbols represent chord names (implied harmony) respective to capoed guitar.
Capoed fret is "0" in tab.

**Chords strummed w/ thumb throughout.

Verses

All nine nine-measure verses are composed of four two-measure increments and a one-measure ending that resolves to the I chord (C). None are exactly alike, making for a progression designed to hold the interest despite the repetition. Be sure to check out measures 5–6, where Johnson deviates from the mostly eighth notes with a sustained C7 for three beats of stop-time (measure 5) and dotted quarter notes (measure 6). These two measures almost functions as a short bridge, making the last three measures go by in a burst of energy.

They're Red Hot
Verse

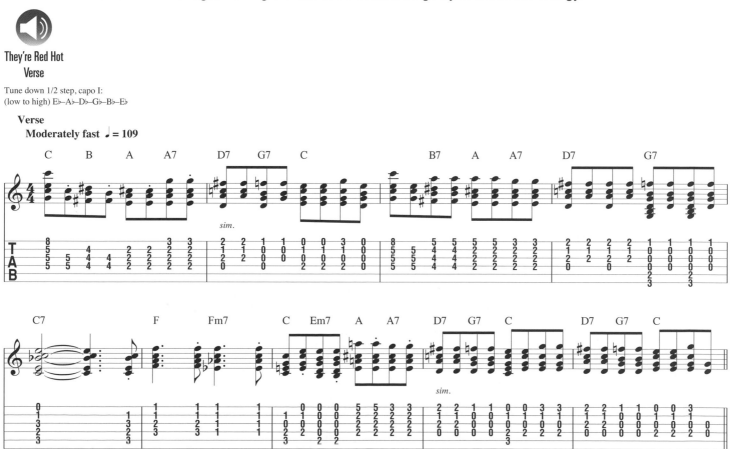

Walkin' Blues
Recorded Friday, November 27, 1936, in San Antonio, Texas

Based on the 12-bar blues "My Black Mama" by Son House, an "axe fall" blues so-called because it reflected a work song in which two men synchronized the swing of their axes by hitting on the downbeat. The steady quarter notes have also been likened to someone walking, hence the title. With all due respect to the equally legendary Eddie House, Johnson's version is musically superior due to his steady, pulsing groove, the lilt he adds to his rhythm, and the virtuosic fretted licks he occasionally plays over the IV and V chords. Where House played steadily occurring slide notes over his strummed rhythm and references his mother's death as the cause of his "blues," Johnson is sparing with his slide and makes part of his story a defiance of death.

Verse 3

As opposed to verses 1 and 2 (not shown), where he stays on the bass strings for his accompaniment, Johnson keeps busy in verse 3 as he flaunts his chops. Besides the metronomic beat and the tender way he lightly touches the tonic note (A) at fret 5 of string 1 with his slide in between the downbeats of the I chord, he plays remarkably modern-sounding licks over the IV chord (D7) in measures 5–6 and 10 and the V chord (E7) in measure 9.

Performance Tip: Be sure to angle the slide away from string 2 and the ones below when accessing the A note on string 1. Barre with the index finger at frets 5 and 7 to play the hot licks over the IV and V chords, respectively (see photo).

Walkin' Blues
Verse 3

Open A tuning, down 1/2 step, capo II:
(low to high) E♭–A♭–E♭–A♭–C–E♭

*Symbols represent chord names (implied harmony) respective to capoed guitar.
Capoed fret is "0" in tab.

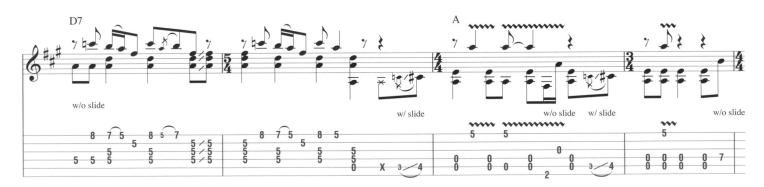

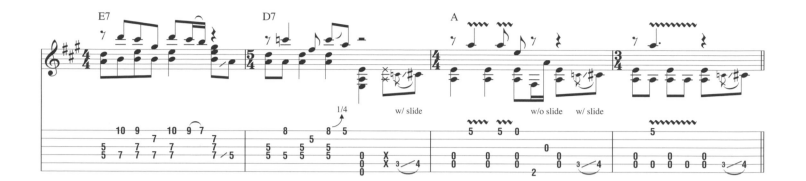

Verse 5, Measures 11–12

Johnson extends his creativity to the last two measures of the tune with a recap of his open-A slide dyad at fret 12, E/C♯, as heard in the intro (not shown). Following the dyad is an A major arpeggio—A (root), C♯ (3rd), and E (5th)—that is also delineated with the slide. The phrase ends with the A note at fret 5 of string 1 and a pair of open bass strings, A (string 5) and E (string 4).

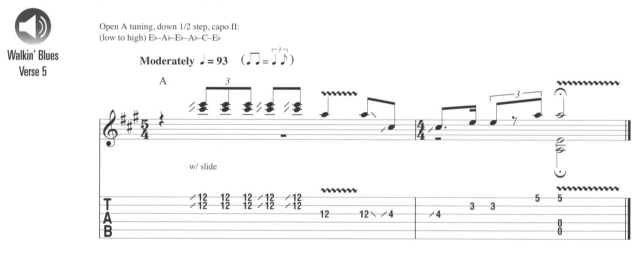

Walkin' Blues
Verse 5

Open A tuning, down 1/2 step, capo II:
(low to high) E♭–A♭–E♭–A♭–C–E♭

Moderately ♩ = 93

Preachin' Blues (Up Jumped the Devil)
Recorded Friday, November 27, 1936, in San Antonio, Texas

Another classic track inspired by a Son House recording and a virtuosic performance by one of the first guitar heroes. House actually *was* a preacher at a point early on, but it is the secular Johnson who delivers the "fire and brimstone" while throwing down the musical gauntlet to anyone brave enough to attempt this masterpiece. Which means… pick it up (your guitar) and accept the challenge!

Intro

Next to "Ramblin' on My Mind," "Preachin' Blues" is the only other Johnson song in open E tuning. Consequently, there are similarities in the phrasing of the first-inversion triad riff at fret 12 preceding his ubiquitous descending intro turnaround, albeit at a brisker tempo. However, in a manner befitting a landmark innovative Delta blues, Johnson dramatically and dynamically transitions to his spectacular, "head cutting," monochord slide riffs.

Performance Tip: One of the most difficult slide techniques is quickly interspersing slide licks on the top three strings—or just the high E string—among open bass strings or fretted licks. As in the performance tip for verse 3 of "Walkin' Blues," it is absolutely paramount to angle the slide away from the middle and lower strings, taking care to only cover the appropriate ones.

Preachin' Blues
Intro

Open E tuning, down 1/2 step:
(low to high) E♭–B♭–E♭–G–B♭–E♭

Verse 1, Measures 11–12

As he does on occasion throughout, Johnson dynamically drops his slider down on the bass strings to execute the bluesy C♯ (6th)–E (root) and D (♭7th)–E licks on strings 5 and 4 in measures 11 and 12, respectively.

Preachin' Blues
Verse 1

Open E tuning, down 1/2 step:
(low to high) E♭–B♭–E♭–G–B♭–E♭

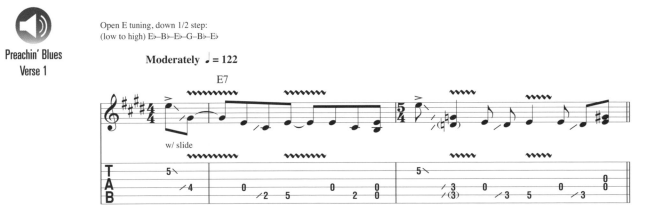

Verse 2, Measure 1

Johnson knew the importance of adding variety to a repetitive song. In measure 1 of verse 2, he interrupted his slashing slide to rapidly strum (16th notes) strings 5–1 open in a dramatic flurry of sound.

Performance Tip: Johnson likely used his thumb pick like a flatpick, employing up and downstrokes. If utilizing bare fingers, it is recommended to either alternate down and upstrokes with the thumb and index finger, respectively, or to employ the thumb like a plectrum.

Preachin' Blues
Verse 2, m. 1

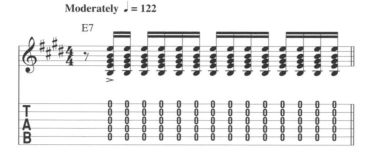

Verse 2, Measures 8–10

Would it really be a legitimate blues without the classic ♭3rd–♮3rd–root lick inserted somewhere? In measures 8–10, Johnson uses his slide to play G–G♯, followed by E on the open first string or at fret 5 of string 2.

Preachin' Blues
Verse 2, m. 8–10

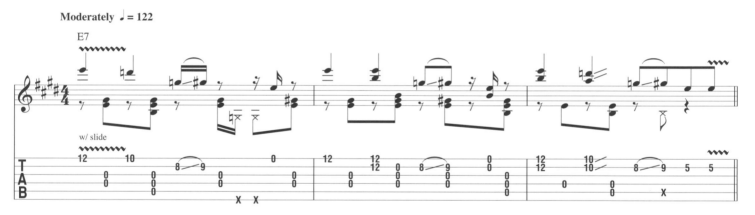

Verse 2, Measure 14

Mid-measure, Johnson slips in a slick fretted chordal move of G♯/D (3rd/♭7th) on strings 1 and 2 combined with a pull-off to the open first string (E), thereby indicating a quick E7 tonality.

Performance Tip: Low to high, use the index and middle fingers for G♯/D.

Preachin' Blues
Verse 2, m. 14

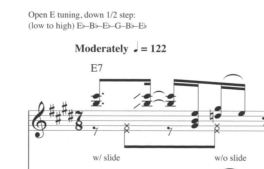

Verse 5, Measure 13

Under his climactic lyric of "Goin' to the 'stil'ry" (followed by "stay out there all day" in measure 14), Johnson sneaks in another classic blues lick, with fretted D and C# notes followed by a slide to the root, E.

Performance Tip: Utilize the middle and index fingers for the fretted notes on string 5.

I'm a Steady Rollin' Man (Steady Rollin' Man)
Recorded Saturday, June 19, 1937, in Dallas, Texas

If there is one Robert Johnson song that should be at the top of any guitarist's list to learn for a host of technical and aesthetic reasons, it is "I'm a Steady Rollin' Man." Played in standard tuning without a capo, both unusual for Johnson, the slow-change 12-bar blues features a boogie shuffle groove that was a template for countless future electric blues songs to come.

Intro

It is impossible to know too many of Johnson's four-measure "double turnaround" intros. This one, like the three-measure intro in "Kind Hearted Woman Blues," is a keeper. In "real time," the two intros actually even out, as "Steady Rollin' Man" contains a measure in 2/4 time, while "Kind Hearted Woman" contains a measure in 6/4 time.

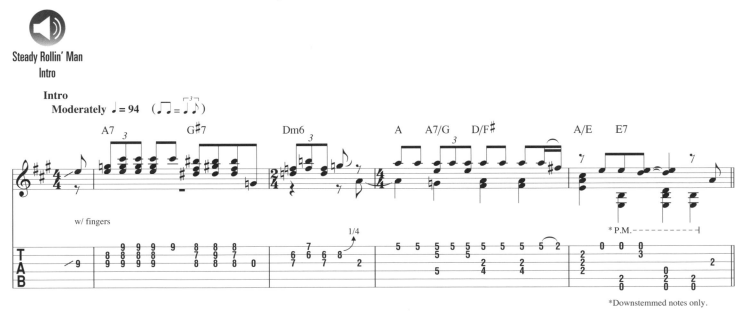

Verse 1

Inasmuch as playing in standard tuning does not afford Johnson the amount of easily accessible major-chord tones found in open tuning, Johnson is compelled to select his notes with even more care to avoid unwanted dissonances. In fact, it provides another opportunity for him to display his uncanny skill at choosing prime combinations of bass and treble string notes, leaving the middle register dynamically hollow for the ear to subconsciously fill in.

The entire verse is packed full of signature licks. However, take special note of the following:

Measures 1–2 (I chord): The A note (root) on fret 5 of string 1 rings out like a chime, two octaves above the open fifth string. The classic bass-string embellishment on beat 4 of measure 1 is a required part of the blues curriculum—and you will be tested!

Steady Rollin' Man
Verse 1, m. 1–2

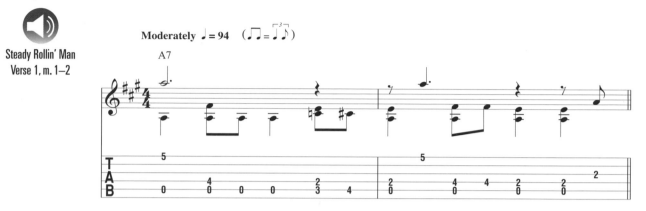

Measures 5–6 (IV chord): Though based on a garden-variety D7 chord derived from an open-position C7 fingering, the picking pattern has a propulsive rolling effect. In addition, keeping the high A (5th) on string 1 creates a common tone between the I and IV chord changes to produce a smooth transition.

Performance Tip: Finger the D7, low to high, with the ring, middle, index, and pinky. Lift the ring finger up to access the open fifth string where notated.

Steady Rollin' Man
Verse 1, m. 5–6

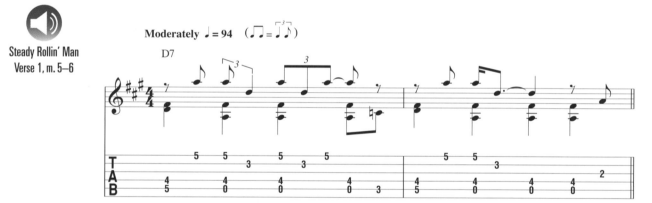

Measures 7–8 (I chord): A true highlight occurs in measures 7–8. While maintaining his steady quarter-note and eighth-note pulse on the bottom strings, Johnson simultaneously injects two descending A blues scale runs, and it is no mean feat!

Performance Tip: Barre across fret 2 with the index finger as if playing an A major chord. Use the pinky and middle fingers to access the runs.

Steady Rollin' Man
Verse 1, m. 7–8

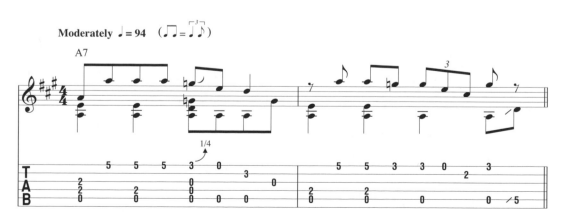

Measure 9 (V chord): Johnson once again proves the inherent power of (mostly) just two notes: low E (root) and high B (5th), and then low B and high B.

Performance Tip: Use your ring finger for the low E and low B, and your pinky for the high B. Add the E on string 2 with the index finger. Use the ring finger as a small barre to play E/B on the bass strings.

Steady Rollin' Man
Verse 1, m. 9

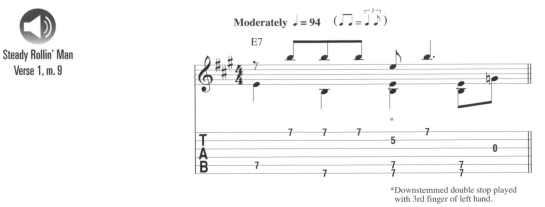

*Downstemmed double stop played
with 3rd finger of left hand.

From Four Until Late
Recorded Saturday, June 19, 1937, in Dallas, Texas

Johnson's only other song in the key of C, "From Four Until Late" is based on the music of a subgenre called "Betty & Dupree" tunes. It is also reminiscent of an aspect of Lonnie Johnson, as well as ragtime, while being a long way from Delta blues. "From Four Until Late" is the closest he ever came to recording a "pop" song and gives a tantalizing hint of the breadth of material he was said to have performed live.

Note: In verse 2, Johnson states "From Memphis to Norfolk is a 36-hour ride." The actual distance is approximately 800 miles, computing to an average speed of 22 MPH, slow even for the '30s, decades before the advent of the Interstate Highway System!

Intro

Johnson plays measures 1 and 2 of the descending "double turnaround" in his standard fashion, but takes a "turn" to what could be seen as proto-Kansas City jazz in measures 3–4, as he swings the chords like a big-band guitarist. Note the atypical country-blues G7 voicing (B–F–G–B, low to high) on beat 2 in measure 4 (see photo).

Performance Tip: The secret to making measures 3 and 4 swing effortlessly is to alternate downstrokes and upstrokes with the thumb and index finger, respectively, beginning on beat 1 of measure 3.

From Four Until Late
Intro

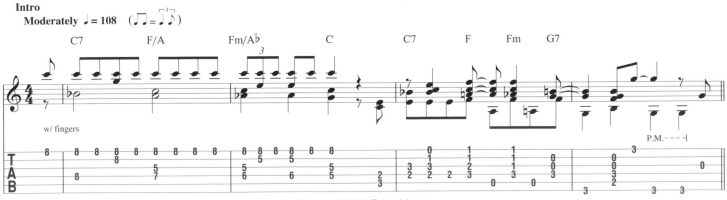

Verse 3

Though they are all similar, a compendium of hip blues guitar licks and riffs may be found in verse 3, which contains this classic Johnson line: "A woman is like a dresser, some man always ramblin' through its drawers." In measure 2 (IV chord, F), Johnson walks down from fret 8 with unusual dyads—C/E♭, B/D, A/C, F♯/A, and E/G—played approximately in unison with his vocal line. The lower harmony notes—E♭ (♭7th), D (6th), C (5th), and A (3rd)—could be seen as derived from the F Mixolydian mode. However, the upper melody notes—C, B (♭5th), A, F♯ (♭9th), and E (major 7th)—may very well have been a matter of expediency with respect to fingering, though the C and A notes are also sung. Further analysis reveals that he is also singing the D and G notes found in the harmony line. At any rate, it sounds great in context!

Measure 3 (and measure 7, similarly), played over the C (I) chord, shows his Lonnie Johnson influence. A descending pattern containing dyads in 3rds on strings 2 and 1—G/E (5th/3rd), G♭/E♭ (♭5th/♭3rd), F/D (4th/9th), and E/C (3rd/root)—leads logically to the C7 change in measure 4.

In measure 5 (IV chord), Johnson adds the G note on string 1 to the F major triad for a brief extension of the harmony (Fadd9). He also adds it in measure 6 (iv chord, Fm7), implying Fm9.

From Four Until Late
Verse 3

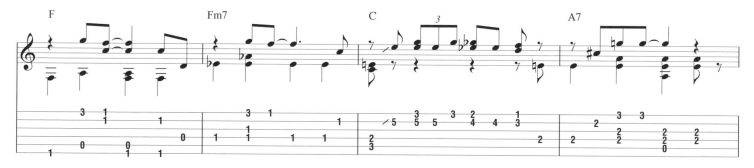

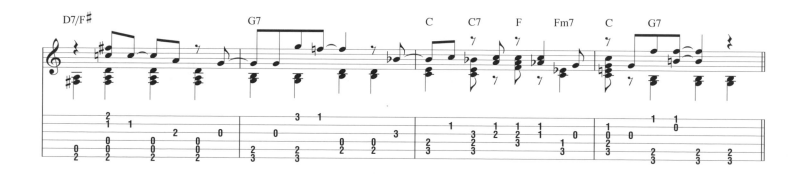

Hell Hound on My Trail
Recorded Sunday, June 20, 1937, in Dallas, Texas

The first song recorded on the last day of his last session, "Hell Hound on My Trail" is his most idiosyncratic arrangement. It's also his only recorded track in open E minor tuning. Johnson likely learned the tuning from Johnny Temple, who is famously acknowledged for recording the first cut boogie song, "Lead Pencil Blues," in G major in 1935. Temple had picked up the minor tuning from Skip James, who was known for playing in D minor, as heard prominently in "Devil Got My Woman" and "Yola My Blues Away." Along with "Me and the Devil Blues" and, to an extent, "Crossroads," "Hell Hound on My Trail" has contributed to Johnson's mythology.

Note: Be aware that Johnson actually implies major or dominant I, IV, and V chords rather than minor ones.

Intro

Due to strings 3–1 being tuned the same as standard tuning, descending major-key turnaround patterns with triple stops on those strings may be utilized, as seen beginning on E7 (I chord) in measure 1 and ending on E7 in measure 4. In reality, the only strings which deviate from standard are 5 (B) and 4 (E).

Performance Tip: Observe the descending bass line on string 5, plucked in conjunction with the open second (B) and first (E) strings, to create an effect similar to open E tuning in "Ramblin' on My Mind." The result makes the ♭3rd (G) prominence in the verses all the more melancholy and dramatic.

Hell Hound
Intro

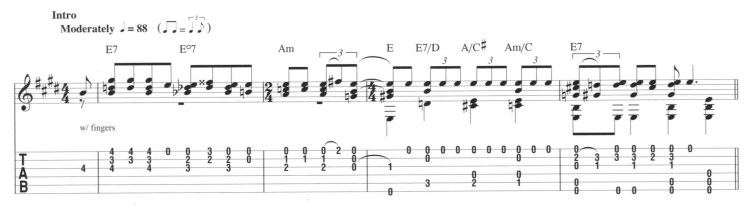

Verse 2

Johnson was a master of the sonically dramatic "hollow" sound of sparse treble and bass notes implying more then was actually played. "Hell Hound on My Trail" is his ultimate example, while additionally containing the only recording featuring him singing in unison with his riffs (measures 1–2 in verses 1, 2, and 4).

In measures 1–3 of verse 2, over E and B7 changes, he literally just picks the "train whistles" B/G (5th/♭3rd) and A/F (♭7th/♭5th), respectively, with the ♭3rd and ♭5th (G and F) bent a quarter step to the "true blue note." Not until measures 4–5 does he get the bass and treble divide working in what would be a type of turnaround resolving to the I chord (E) if it appeared in the last two measures of the verse. In fact, Johnson does indeed incorporate the concept as a "double turnaround" in measures 12–14.

Performance Tip: Be aware that, as in the intro, the turnaround does not resolve to the V chord (B7) as is most typical in the blues, but instead to the I chord (E).

Hell Hound
Verse 2

Open Em tuning:
(low to high) E–B–E–G–B–E

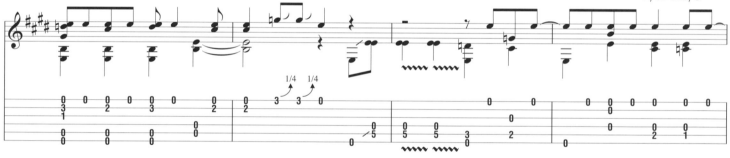

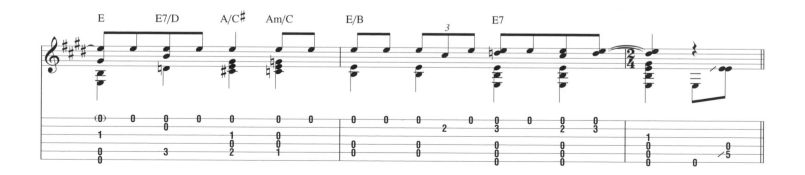

Stop Breakin' Down Blues
Recorded Sunday, June 20, 1937, in Dallas, Texas

It would be difficult to overestimate the pervasive influence this chugging shuffle would have on postwar Chicago blues and, by extension, rock 'n' roll. Covers by Junior Wells and none other than the Rolling Stones attest to its timeless appeal. Like other tracks from Johnson's last recording session, "Stop Breakin' Down Blues" stands alone from the rest of his oeuvre in that it is the only non-slide number in open A tuning. In addition, it gains its shuffle power through rhythmic means other than cut boogie patterns.

Intro

As opposed to several of his other songs, Johnson opted for a standard two-measure intro containing his typical descending pattern resolving to the I chord (A). The brisk tempo (115 BPM) marches right into verse 1 in a pulse-racing display of blues-fired energy.

Performance Tip: Note the root (A), ♭3rd (C), and major 3rd (C♯) bass run on beats 3 and 4 of measure 2. A classic boogie blues embellishment, it also appears in measures at the end of each verse, except for verse 4 (which may have been a mistake), as a way to boost momentum.

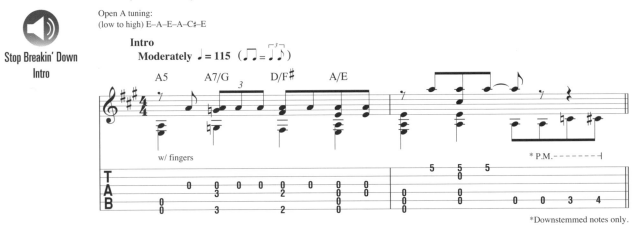

Verse 1

Check out how, in measures 1–3 of each verse, Johnson inserts the intro boogie bass embellishment as a "pickup" into the next measure. Also not to be missed is the way he includes at least one note on string 1 in each measure as a way of maintaining continuity. Besides that, it makes for a ringing, moving melody in the upper register, which contrasts dynamically with the loping shuffle rhythm.

Performance Tip: Observe the way the melody notes on string 1 are either the root of the I chord (A), the ♭7th (G) of the I7 chord (A7), or the ♭7th (C) of the IV7 (D7) chord. In other words, they help to bring out the defining quality of those changes.

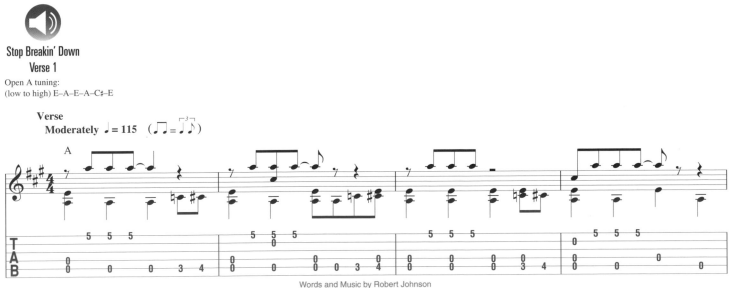

Love in Vain Blues
Recorded Sunday, June 20, 1937, in Dallas, Texas

Unfortunately, "Love in Vain Blues" is better-known to many rock fans because of the credible Rolling Stones version. Nonetheless, it contains some of Johnson's most poetically melancholy lyrics, as well as being his only known composition in open G tuning. Owners of the compilation CDs will be aware of the amazing snippet of his recorded speaking voice saying, "I wanna go on with our next one myself."

Intro

Though his four-measure intro sounds like typical Johnson fare on first listen, closer examination reveals a harmony in measures 1–2 that is unique to the track. Taking advantage of the open G tuning, with the greatest efficiency and economy of means, he plays the top two strings in 3rds in the upper register to imply G, G°7, and D7 before dynamically dropping down the fretboard for his "standard" G–G7/F–C/E–Cm/E♭–D7 pattern.

Performance Tip: Pay close attention to the phrasing, which is neither typical nor standard for Johnson. In measure 1, he does play four groups of triplets. However, he alternates steady strumming on beats 1 and 3 with syncopated rests on beats 2 and 4 for a unique feel. Measure 2, in 2/4 time, momentarily halts the forward momentum in subtle musical expression of the pathos that follows lyrically in the verses.

Love in Vain
Intro

Open G tuning, up 1/2 step:
(low to high) D♯–G♯–D♯–G♯–B♯–D♯

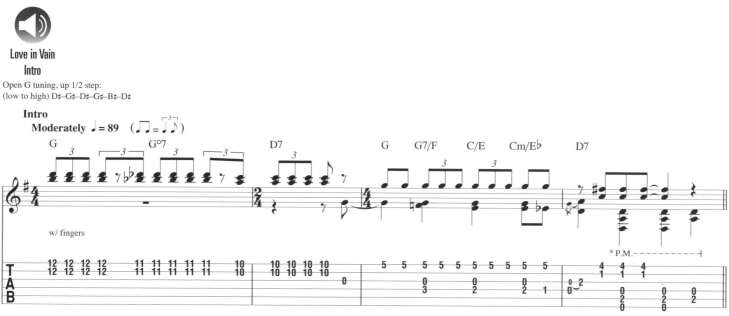

*Downstemmed notes only.

Verse 1

Johnson arranged this 12-bar blues' verses to contain a jazzy II–V–I sequence (A7–D7–G) in measures 9–11, a progression previously encountered only in "They're Red Hot" and "From Four Until Late." One of the signature licks, which he repeats in each verse, occurs between beat 4 of measure 2 and beat 1 of measure 3. Involving a slide that creates a D/G dyad leading to a big, vibrant G7 voicing (high to low: F–D–G–D–B, or ♭7th–5th–root–5th–3rd), the lick commands the overarching tonality of the verse, reinforced in measure 4. Similarly, in measure 7, he connects G7 (I) to D7 (V) with graceful broken chords, followed by a sustained, ringing G and B in measure 8.

Performance Tip: Be aware that the V chord may be inserted for two beats (3 and 4) into a measure of the I chord in many different musical genres but is especially welcome in the blues due to the harmonic variety and forward motion it provides.

Love in Vain
Verse 1

Open G tuning, up 1/2 step:
(low to high) D♯–G♯–D♯–G♯–B♯–D♯

*Barre your index finger at the 2nd fret each time you play the C chord.

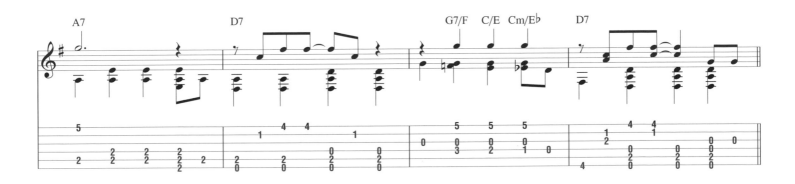

INTEGRAL TECHNIQUES

Johnson Fingerstyle

From videos and the reminiscence of first-hand accounts, we know country blues guitarists such as Mississippi John Hurt and the Rev. Gary Davis picked with their right-hand thumbs and index fingers. Others utilized the thumb in conjunction with the index and middle fingers. All we can say with certainty about the picking technique of Johnson is that he employed a plastic thumb pick, as seen in the "Pinstripe Suit" studio photo. However, the audio evidence strongly suggests that he would sometimes use it as a flatpick for extra volume and clarity on the treble strings, as well as to thump the bass strings. As a general guideline, however, think thumb on strings 6, 5, and 4 and a combination of the index and middle fingers on strings 3, 2, and 1. As opposed to classical and flamenco guitarists who play with all five right-hand fingers in a very prescribed way, blues, folk, and rock guitarists tend to freely pick with the thumb, index, and middle fingers in a manner that feels most natural.

While Johnson often employed standard dominant chord voicings, his phrasing just as often lifted them out of the mundane. The following intro suggests a downstroke with the thumb on beat 1, followed by the index and middle fingers on strings 2 and 1, respectively, for the A7 chord. On beat 3, again use a downstroke on the bass strings and then pick upward with the index for B/A.

Techniques
Example 1

Our next example is essentially the first measure of the turnaround in a 13-measure verse: after picking with the thumb on string 6, it seems prudent to use the thumb, index, and middle fingers for the broken E7 chord on beat 2. A downstroke with the thumb for Db/Bb on beat 3 would work well, while the thumb and index, used in a plucking motion, could be utilized for the notes on strings 3 and 1 on beat 4.

Techniques
Example 2

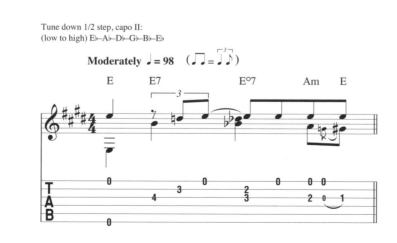

Below is another example of where it makes good sense to employ the thumb on the upper strings. In the opening pickup measure, pick the E note on string 3 with the thumb and use the middle finger on string 1 and the index finger for string 2. In measure 1, turn the thumb into a flatpick and brush downward on strings 3, 2, and 1 on beat 1. Likewise, on beat 2, pick the bent C note on string 3 with the thumb, followed by the index on string 1 with an upstroke. On beat 4, employ the thumb on strings 6 and 5 and simultaneously pick upward with the index on string 2, followed by a pluck with the middle finger on string 1.

Techniques Example 3

For this example, use straight downstroke strumming with the thumb. Regarding the C note on string 2 in measure 1: it is possible that Johnson actually fingered a full D7/F♯ voicing, but only applied pressure to the C note on the beat 2 strum. In measure 2, however, he may have nicked the C note with an up-pick of his index finger.

Techniques Example 4

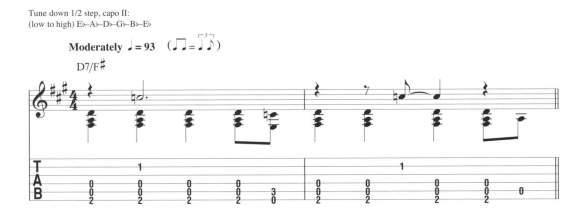

The following example's challenging phrasing showcases Johnson's vaunted chops. Use the thumb on the bass strings, as usual, and the index finger on string 1.

Techniques Example 5

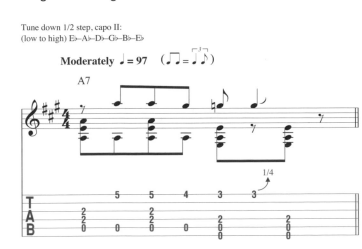

The composite blues scale riffs in this next example are ahead of their time and worthy of Lonnie Johnson! Utilize your right hand's middle finger on string 1 and the index finger on string 2.

**Techniques
Example 6**

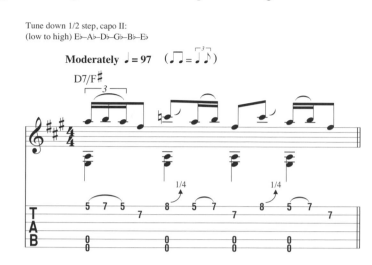

Johnson likes to rake a fast arpeggio on occasion, as heard on the upbeat of beat 1. Use the index to quickly roll across the strings for a bell-like effect.

**Techniques
Example 7**

Johnson often employed the percussive kick of palm-muted strings. Here, he contrasts the open fifth string (A), accessed with the thumb pick, against the sustained and vibratoed A note on string 1 for dynamic expression. Be sure to angle the slider away from the fingerboard so as to only touch string 1.

**Techniques
Example 8**

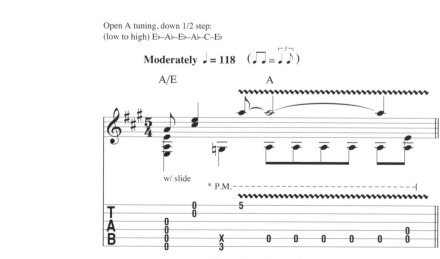

*Downstemmed notes only.

Johnson did a credible Lonnie Johnson tribute in one of his only two compositions in drop D tuning. With the sparest of elements, he swings the lesser classic blues bend of the 2nd (E) to the ♭3rd (F), followed by dyads and single notes related to a second-position D major triad.

**Techniques
Example 9**

Equally spare as the previous example, this one contains deep and vibrant bass-string licks, highlighted by the sassy quarter-step bend of the F (♭3rd) to the "true blue note" in between the ♭3rd and major 3rd.

**Techniques
Example 10**

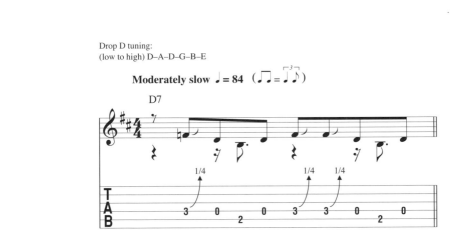

Here, Johnson channels Lonnie Johnson with funky dyads in 3rds, creating anticipation that leads to resolution on a hip D7 triple stop.

**Techniques
Example 11**

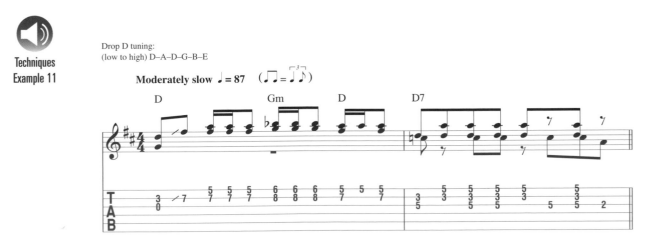

It appears to be a standard Johnson descending, diminished turnaround until a closer look reveals the subtle alterations of harmony and phrasing. Notice the "time-altering" transition from measure 2 to measure 3 involving the A (root), C♯ (3rd), and A (octave) notes. Also, check out the addition of the E (5th) in measure 3, which is played by barring strings 2 and 1 with the pinky while leaving the index at fret 2—if your fingers are as long as his!

Techniques
Example 12

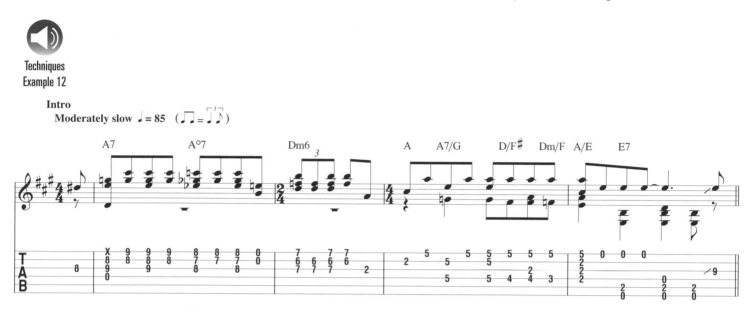

As indicated below the notation, the A7 triple stop in measure 2 must be voiced with the ring, middle, and pinky fingers, low to high, in order to quickly access it following the bass-string figure in measure 1 (see photo). Not for the faint of heart!

*Fretted with ring, middle & pinky fingers (low to high).

Barre Chords

Regarding the left hand: though blues guitar tradition dictates Johnson must have wrapped his thumb over the low E string—and perhaps even the A string sometimes—he also clearly barred with his index finger (see "Pinstripe Suit" studio photo).

On beat 1, barre strings 3–1 at fret 5 with the index finger while placing the ring finger on string 4 at fret 7 and the middle finger on string 3 at fret 6.

Techniques Example 14

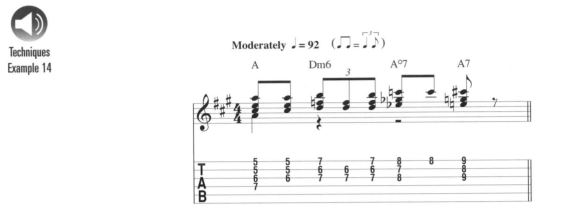

Barre strings 4–1 at fret 2 with the index finger, being careful to preserve the open fifth string. Use the middle (or ring) finger to access the G note on fret 3 of string 1.

Techniques Example 15

Barre strings 4–1 at fret 2 with the index, placing the pinky on string 1 at fret 5.

Techniques Example 16

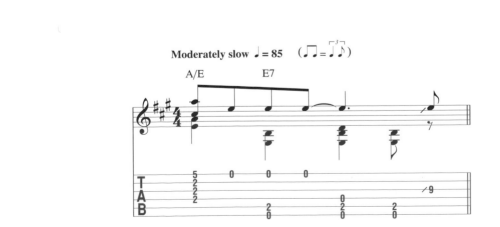

As exists in all the common open tunings, barring across fret 5 creates the IV chord as a major voicing. Barre strings 5–1 with the index finger. Be aware, however, that the root note appears on string 5, not 6, in open A and open G.

Techniques
Example 17

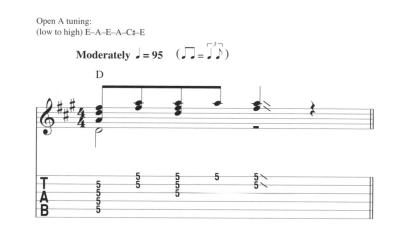

Slide Guitar

Johnson could move seamlessly between slide and fretted licks and riffs, so let's check out an entire eight-bar verse to see this stunning skill in action. Pay particular attention to the measures in which he simultaneously strums bass notes with his thumb (pick) while picking the slide notes with his index finger. As previously mentioned, this technique requires precise positioning of the slider so as not to mute the fretted and open bass-string chord forms, as seen in measures 3–4 and 6.

Techniques
Example 18

Though he could sound like a whole string band all by himself, Johnson was not averse to repeating simple slide riffs in steady eighth notes to create musical tension. Observe the subtle insertion of the D note (4th) on the upbeat of beat 4 of measure 1, bookended by the classic E/C♯ (5th/3rd) dyad in open A tuning.

**Techniques
Example 19**

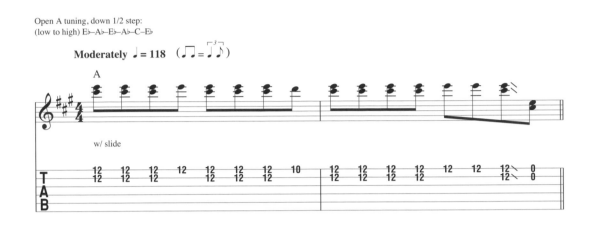

It cannot be reiterated too many times: the blues, and indeed music in any genre, consists of elements of musical tension contrasted with resolution. Observe beats 1 and 2, where the A triad (E–C♯–A: 5th–3rd–root) on the open first, second, and third strings is combined with G–E–C (♭7th–5th–♭3rd) at fret 3.

**Techniques
Example 20**

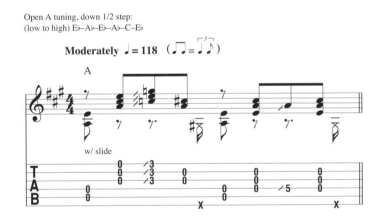

With bold dynamics, Johnson nails E7♯9 with the open E (root) and G (♭3rd) at fret 3, followed by merely the A note (5th) with the slide to imply the D7 chord in an ultimate "less is more" move.

**Techniques
Example 21**

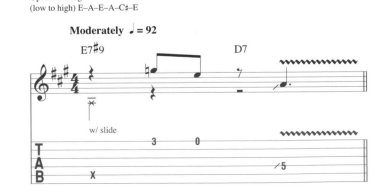

STYLISTIC DNA

By developing and recording at the end of the acoustic country-blues era, Robert Johnson summed up virtually all that was significant in the music while adding his own incalculable contribution.

Fretted Fills

On beat 4 of measure 2, Johnson embellishes the Dm/F chord with a quick hammer-on and pull-off, creating tension and release. It may be an unforgivable pun to say "the devil is in the details," but he knew how to complete a phrase with significant nuance.

DNA
Example 1

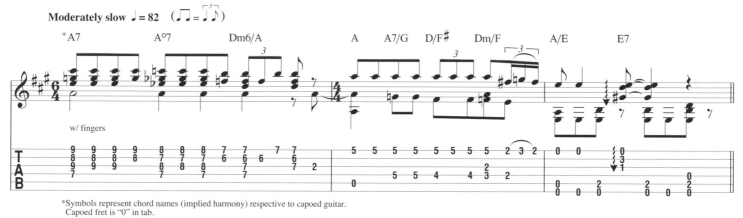

*Symbols represent chord names (implied harmony) respective to capoed guitar.
Capoed fret is "0" in tab.

He did not invent it, but Johnson included the half-step bend on beat 2 whenever he could, proving his blues bonafides.

Performance Tip: Bend the C note on string 3 with the middle finger while holding down the A note on string 1 with the ring finger (see photo).

DNA
Example 2

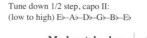

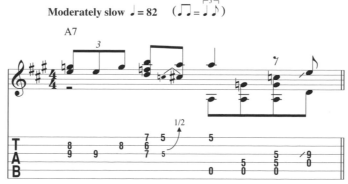

On the upbeat of beat 4, Johnson hammers from the ♭3rd (G, open third string) to the major 3rd (G♯, fret 1) while sustaining the root (E, open first string) to confirm the E major harmony in a bedrock blues lick.

DNA

Example 3

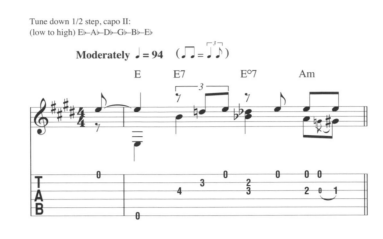

Check out one of the chief advantages of Aadd9 tuning: the root (B) and 5th (F♯) are on strings 6 and 5, respectively, and the upper strings allow simultaneous access to the 3rd (D♯), ♭7th (A), and 9th (C♯) of the B7 (V) chord.

Performance Tip: An advanced technique for an advanced blues tune! Make a small barre on strings 6 and 5 with the middle finger, using the index for fret 6 on string 3 and the ring finger for fret 8 on string 2. The pinky may then play fret 9 on string 1 (see photo).

DNA

Example 4

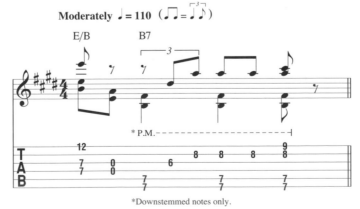

*Downstemmed notes only.

Interspersed with a boogie bass-string pattern for the IV chord (A7) are dynamic treble-string notes from the A Mixolydian mode.

Performance Tip: Anchor the index finger on the root (A) at fret 5 of string 6, utilizing the ring finger for the 5th (E) on string 5. Employ the pinky for the A and C♯ notes, and the ring finger for the B and E notes on beat 4.

DNA
Example 5

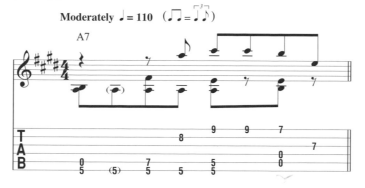

Following the quick hit on D/A (beat 1), Johnson anchors his index finger at fret 7 as a small barre for the V chord (E7), creating various combinations of G♯/E/B (3rd/root/5th) while adding D (♭7th), C♯ (6th), and B (5th) on string 1.

Performance Tip: Use the pinky and ring finger to access D and C♯, respectively.

DNA
Example 6

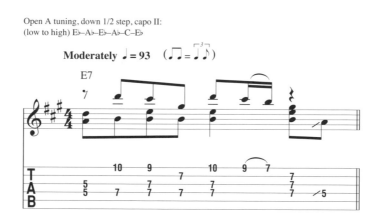

Because he utilized a thumb pick, Johnson could extract sharply-defined, percussive bass-string notes from his resonant guitars. However, whether or not to go with the bare thumb or a pick comes down to personal taste.

Performance Tip: There is room for differing opinions with regard to fingering these types of licks, but the index and middle are suggested.

DNA
Example 7

MUST HEAR

The 29 songs originally pressed on 78 RPM lacquer platters were released on two 33-1/3 RPM vinyl disks in the '60s, while having apparently been sped up in the engineering process. Since then, beginning in 1990, CD box sets from Sony/Columbia containing all the available takes have been issued at various intervals, each purporting to be more accurate with respect to original pitch. All are of value, but the most recent is recommended if only purchasing one.

Robert Johnson: The Complete Recordings, 1990

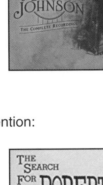

Robert Johnson: The Complete Recordings, 2011

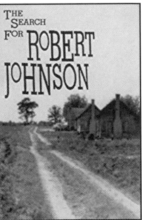

MUST SEE

Besides the known photos, we can only wish for film! However, two biopics are worthy of mention:

The Search for Robert Johnson (with John Hammond), Amazon Video

Can't You Hear the Wind Howl: The Life & Music of Robert Johnson (with Keb Mo') Amazon Video